HV6322 .7G46Y92

GENOCIDE WATCH

NO AUTHOR

P9-DTM-988

DATE DUE

WITHDRAWN

Genocide Watch

Edited by Helen Fein

GENOCIDE

Yale University Press

New Haven

London

WATCH

Copyright © 1992 by Helen Fein. All rights reserved. This book may not be reproduced, in whole or in part, including illustrations, in any form (beyond that copying permitted by Sections 107 and 108 of the U.S. Copyright Law and except by reviewers for the public press), without written permission from the publishers.

Designed by Nancy Ovedovitz and set in Galliard type and printed in the United States of America by The Maple-Vail Book Manufacturing Group, Binghamton, New York.

Library of Congress Cataloging-in-Publication Data

Genocide watch / edited by Helen Fein.

   p. cm.

   ISBN 0-300-04801-7 (alk. paper)

   1. Genocide—Congresses.   I. Fein, Helen, 1934–

HV6322.7.G46   1992

304.6′63—dc20

91-18851

CIP

The paper in this book meets the guidelines for permanence and durability of the Committee on Production Guidelines for Book Longevity of the Council on Library Resources.

10   9   8   7   6   5   4   3   2   1

To Orlanda Brugnola

Contents

This volume reflects the record of a conference which would not have taken place without the commitment of the Institute for the Study of Genocide officers and board, the active participation of Orlanda Brugnola (president of the ISG) and Herbert F. Spirer (vice president), and the facilities of the John Jay College for Criminal Justice.

Besides the authors of this volume, other conference participants who contributed talks or discussions that also shaped our intellectual collaboration include Lloyd Binagi (University of Wisconsin), David Burgess (U.S. State Department Bureau of Human Rights and Humanitarian Affairs), Frank Chalk (Concordia Institute for Genocide Studies), Richard Cohen *(Washington Post)*, Roberta Cohen (Refugee Policy Group), Patricia Weiss Fagen (U.N. High Commissioner for Refugees), Jack Geiger, M.D. (City University of New York), David Hawk (Cambodia Documentation Commission), Mab Huang (State University of New York College at Oswego), Thomas D. Lobe (University of South Dakota), André Maislinger (University of Innsbruck), George Lopez

(University of Notre Dame), Stephen P. Marks (Cardoza Law School), Richard Mollica, M.D. (Harvard University Program in Refugee Trauma), Herbert F. Spirer (University of Connecticut, Stamford), Morton Winston (Trenton State College), and Roger Winter (U.S. Committee for Refugees).

We—the contributors and I—are all indebted to the good judgment, serious commitment, and patience of Yale University Press, and particularly to the intelligence and good humor of our editor Gladys Topkis. Eliza Childs served as an efficient and versatile production editor. We especially appreciated the careful and thoughtful work of the manuscript editor, Cecile Rhinehart Watters, which greatly improved the style and clarity of the book.

During the year this book was edited, I served as a visiting scholar in the Program for Nonviolent Sanctions of the Center for International Affairs of Harvard University. The conclusions gleaned from my research there, supported by a fellowship grant from the Social Science Research Council MacArthur Foundation Program in International Peace and Security, and events since the conference have undoubtedly influenced my introduction.

Helen Fein

Genocide Watch

Chapter 1

Helen Fein

INTRODUCTION

The chapters in this book are the record of written papers (revised by the authors) from the Genocide Watch conference on how to detect and to deter genocide held on May 22–23, 1989, in New York City. The conference was initiated by the Institute for the Study of Genocide and cosponsored by Cultural Survival, the U.S. Committee for Refugees, and the World Council of Indigenous Peoples. The seventy participants—teachers and students, activists and professional staff of refugee and rights organizations, doctors and journalists—had a common goal. They came in order to understand and learn to anticipate genocides and mass killings; to deter massacres rather than to cope with the symptoms; and to understand the causes of official and public denial, disinterest, and failure to respond. Their concern and the structure of the conference produced high involvement and intensive discussions. It was the first conference I have attended where participants continued to talk (in plenary session) for almost an hour after the social hour was scheduled to begin.

Several themes of the conference are not included in this book because they were presented informally rather than in papers. One of keen topical concern—then and now—was the round table on responsibility for protecting human rights during a future settlement in Cambodia. Speakers included official representatives of Singapore, Vietnam, the U.S. State Department, the Cambodia Documentation Commission, and Save Cambodia, a refugee organization (representatives of China and Thailand were invited but did not come). The dissensus among the officials reflected the dissensus of states' aims and strategies that was exhibited at subsequent international meetings on Cambodia. We shared a sense of helplessness, also engendered by the inaction of the United States, other countries, and the United Nations, which have refused to judge the Khmer Rouge;[1] as Song Chhang, representative of Save Cambodia, said, "We are about to dim the lights and play the Killing Fields again." The judgment on that prediction is still out.

Because the charge of genocide is often applied rhetorically to gain attention for different causes, we began by asking: what is genocide in law and in social theory—how is it defined? Both Barbara Harff and Kurt Jonassohn find the definition of the U.N. Genocide Convention (hereafter, UNGC) wanting, for several reasons. Article II reads:

In the preset Convention, genocide means any of the following acts committed with intent to destroy, in whole or in part, a national, ethnical, racial or religious group, as such: (a) Killing members of the group; (b) Causing serious bodily or mental harm to members of the group; (c) Deliberately inflicting on the group conditions of life calculated to bring about its physical destruction in whole or in part; (d) Imposing measures intended to prevent births within the group; (e) Forcibly transferring children of the group to another group.

Harff and Jonassohn criticize the UNGC because it applies only to the collectivities specified in Article II: "a national, ethnical, racial or religious group as such." Further, it is either too inclusive or too

---

1. Hurst Hannum, "International Law and the Cambodian Genocide: The Sounds of Silence," *Human Rights Quarterly* 11, no. 1 (1989): 82–138.

exclusive. Harff, arguing for the first, asserts that Article II, clause b, gives "rise to innumerable claims of victimization," most of which are specious and divert attention from ongoing geno/politicides. Jonassohn, in contrast, believes that the UNGC is an impaired instrument with which to prosecute genocide, even were there a political will to do so, because the definition, he says, does not fit any major genocide since 1945. The latter judgment, however, is questionable. David Hawk, director of the Cambodia Documentation Commission, rebutted Jonassohn's conclusion at the conference. Hawk believes that the Cambodian genocide (and others) are covered under the UNGC, that the UNGC definition is workable, and that it is unlikely that social scientists could formulate a clearer definition. In another context, I suggest a social-scientific definition that is consonant with that of the UNGC but broader: "Genocide is sustained purposeful action by a perpetrator to physically destroy a collectivity directly or indirectly, through interdiction of the biological and social reproduction of group members, sustained regardless of the surrender or lack of threat offered by the victim."[2] But since *genocide* is a legal term in international criminal law, neither this nor any other sociological definition will replace it.

The dissensus about the usefulness of the UNGC definition stems in part from the absence of case law; no state has tried anyone for genocide under conditions affording adequate judicial safeguards and reference to provisions of the UNGC. Both Romania and Equatorial Guinea have held trials of their former dictators that included charges of genocide, but neither trial satisfied independent observers. I shall consider later why the UNGC has not been employed and what might be done with it in discussing the chapters by Leo Kuper and Vratislav Pechota.

Although both Harff and Jonassohn developed their definitions for research purposes—to identify contemporary and historical cases—they have different definitions in part because they have different research agendas.

2. Helen Fein, "Genocide: A Sociological Perspective," *Current Sociology* 38, no. 1 (Spring 1990): 24.

Harff (with Ted R. Gurr) focuses on victims of state murders since 1945, attempting to make, for a limited span of time, some difficult distinctions that discriminate genocide from "politicide"—mass murder of groups for political motives or in response to political opposition—despite the evidence that motives are frequently mixed and that opposition is often structured on group lines in societies in which group identity and party identification coincide. In classifying cases, Harff finds many mixed cases, as one would expect (see table 3.1 in her chapter).

Jonassohn (with Frank Chalk) uses definition as a net to unify the likeness among a wide range of cases throughout history, sketching an explanation of how such practices might have evolved. For Jonassohn and Chalk, "genocide is a form of one-sided mass killing in which a state or other authority intends to destroy a group, as that group and membership in it are defined by the perpetrator." The breadth of this definition is problematic for it includes pseudogroups and nongroups—"wreckers" and "enemies of the people" in the twentieth century—rather than real collectivities, sensitizing us to how labeling can kill rather than how and when existing collectivities become subject to destruction.

Although Jonassohn and Harff take different approaches to definition and the criteria differentiating genocide from other state murders and massacres, they agree that the state is the primary perpetrator of genocide. Both also focus on victims killed directly or indirectly rather than by the other means of group destruction enumerated in the UNGC, involving imposed harm, proscription of birth, and forcible transfer of children.

Both agree that mass killing in war, when such killing is within the war convention or internationally agreed rules of war, is not genocide. Harff considers how war crimes and genocide may evolve during wars. Neither counts victims of single massacres or short-term episodes as victims of genocide, Harff excluding episodes lasting less than six months and Jonassohn including only cases in which the group's "victimization threatens its survival as a group." Both distinguish genocide from ethnocide, the elimination of a group's cultural identity without its physical elimination. Both agree that intent to eliminate a group is a primary criterion of genocide, although intent must most often be established on prime facie evidentiary grounds. Both classify political groups as victims, but Harff terms them victims of politicide and Jonassohn terms them victims of genocide. Harff thus discriminates genocide from politicide on the basis of the motive (rather than the intent) of the perpetrator; the UNGC defines genocide in terms of intent regardless of motive.

Both Jonassohn and Harff recognize the difficulty of explaining the apparent irrationality (if viewed solely in terms of material and political costs and gains) of modern ideological genocides: in the Ottoman Empire, in Nazi Germany, and in Kampuchea. Jonassohn considers them the "paradigmatic type" of the twentieth century and compares some competing tentative explanations relating genocide to the legitimation of new regimes and nationalism. Harff relates the likelihood of a government's employment of genocide or severe repression to the form of that government: democracies are least likely to use genocide. Forms of government, ideologies professed by leaders, and past patterns of discrimination are clues to detecting new cases of genocide.

Detecting genocide retrospectively for research purposes is a far simpler task than detecting it in the making. At the conference, Hawk remarked on the need to detect stages of human rights violation that might preface or be early stages of genocide. After the conference, the ISG published such a study: Helen Fein, *Lives at Risk: A Study of Violations of Life-Integrity in 50 States in 1987 Based on the Amnesty International 1988 Report* (New York: ISG, 1990), which distinguishes states that practice mass killings, selective killing, and torture.

Bill Frelick, Vera Beaudin Saeedpour, and René Lemarchand consider how we cull evidence and make inferences in specific cases of genocide. Frelick shows how firsthand testimonies of refugees—likely to flee in cases of genocide unless all exits are blocked—can be systematically gathered and evaluated, conforming to professional standards. Jack Geiger, representative from Physicians for Human Rights, explained how physicians can infer the means and pattern of attack by systematically assessing evidence of bodily injuries among victims (his paper is not included here). This was especially important in the case of the Kurdish victims of gassing in Iraq.

Saeedpour analyzes the geographic pattern of Iraqi gas attacks on the Kurds in 1987–1988 to refute official explanations—and justifications of Iraqi apologists—that the Kurds were attacked in reprisal for the collaboration of some Kurds with Iran during the Iran-Iraq War. In fact, Kurds were gassed and driven to flee in 1988–1989 in areas not adjacent to Iran but bordering Turkey. This is consistent with evidence of long-range Iraqi plans to depopulate Iraqi Kurdistan and to expel the Kurds from an oil-rich zone, replacing them with Arabs. Further, Saeedpour shows from captured documents that the Iraqi plans for depopulation and expulsion are complementary to plans for genocide.

In the spring and summer of 1989, Iraq deported 200,000 more Kurds with virtually no notice in the Western press. Many states have expressed concern about official Iraqi threats to use poison gas against its neighbors, but few persons noted evidence in early 1989 of Iraq's illegal acquisition of biotoxins.

Lemarchand, in a sophisticated and scholarly analysis, shows how the government-organized genocide of Hutus by the Tutsi in Burundi in 1971–1972 differed from the unpremeditated army massacre of Hutus in 1988 and discusses how the latter happened. He refutes both stereotyped explanations of the Tutsi-Hutu conflict and denials of the reality of the conflict. He especially scores the glossing over of such realities by certain academics who disinform and overlook the phenomena they wish to ignore.

Lemarchand shows the interaction of threat and collective retaliation—massacre, pogrom, or genocide—between Tutsi and Hutu and how the persistent memory of the unacknowledged genocide impedes intergroup coexistence today. The memory evoked the fears and rumors that led to the 1988 massacre. Although this is a specific analysis based on Lemarchand's twenty years of research on Burundi and Rwanda, many elements of his analysis pertain to other conflicts and places: the political mobilization of ethnic groups in new states, the domination of the state by one group and systematic curtailment of rights and opportunities of the other, the dominant ethnoclass's fear of a revolutionary takeover by the suppressed ethnoclass, and the official denial of ethnic differences. Such denials serve as ideology, myth, and propaganda for home and foreign consumption.

Before we can respond to genocide and ethnic conflict, we have to recognize them. In large part, our apprehension of genocidal massacres, pogroms, and riots in places remote from the West is a product of the Western media: its focus, continuity of coverage, and labeling. Walter Ezell considers some issues relating to new coverage of genocide and massacres in Africa and the Middle East.

Ezell analyzes how newspapers covered and headlined atrocities in Burundi, Mozambique, and Iraq in 1988 through content analysis of five eminent newspapers in the United States during the critical periods: the pattern of coverage, the instigators that led to news services' reportage, the labeling of cases, the ambiguities introduced, and the policy issues raised. One ambiguity (in Burundi) was failing to note whether the perpetrator of a massacre was an unorganized ethnic group or an organized state force. The former, one suspects, would evoke a very different response than the latter, which clearly indicates official culpability. Another ambiguity that is apt to condition responses is focusing on conflict, thus implying that strife is bilateral, and ignoring one-sided slaughters; these may be pogroms, massacres, or genocide. The newspapers surveyed also tended to give greater credit to government sources than to nongovernment sources, even when the governments were previously involved in genocide or ethnocide—denying the group the right to exist culturally as an entity. This practice discredits the witnesses, converting their experiences to "alleged" atrocities. Ezell concludes that journalists need to investigate such cases more systematically, evaluating refugee testimony critically rather than reproducing it anecdotally and selectively

by presenting speculation about factual matters that can be resolved. . . .
Sophisticated survey methods, which were applied daily, expensively, and
redundantly to predict the outcome of the U.S. presidential elections, could
have been used by the media to understand what was happening in Iraq.
Tens of thousands of refugees were available to be interviewed. Jason Clay
of Cultural Survival and other scholars have developed such techniques for
painting a picture of civil conflict by interviewing refugees, cross-checking
their stories, and using statistical methods to project the results onto a larger
population. It should be possible for a media pool to fly in a trained team
of interviewers, spend days interviewing refugees, and come up with an authoritative conclusion about what is happening inside a country.

To this point, we have not inquired how political biases that diminish or distort perception and evaluation of evidence affect journalists. James E. Mace shows how some prominent American journalists—principally Walter Duranty of the *New York Times*—denied,
and deceived the American public and policymakers in 1932–1933
about, the existence of a famine in the Ukraine created by Joseph
Stalin and his colleagues. Such denials, motivated by both ideological sympathy with what was then conceived as the Soviet "experiment" and opportunism—reporters who echoed what the Politburo
wanted to broadcast won more opportunities to report—had terrible
consequences. Mace observes that "enlightened Americans all the way
up to the president either refused to believe or turned a blind eye to
the famine as they would later to the terror of 1937–1938. Perceptual selectivity based on political conviction, the confusion of fact
and principle such that facts are rejected when inconvenient to one's
political ideals, is as much with us now as it was then."
A contemporary example of this is the refusal of many Western
reporters to credit and transmit the reports of Khmer Rouge atrocities in Cambodia between 1975 and 1979. William Shawcross tells
us that

it was some time before many reporters came to accept that terrible events
were taking place in Cambodia. Just as few people had wished to believe in
the elimination of the Jews until the evidence was thrust before them, so
many people wished not to believe that atrocities were taking place in Cam-

bodia after the Khmer Rouge takeover. This was especially true among reporters who had reported the war negatively from the Lon Nol side, hoping for the victory of the others. Far from eagerly seeking, let alone fabricating, evidence of Khmer Rouge atrocities, they shrank from it. Others believed, at least for a short time, that the refugees were unreliable, that the CIA was cooking up a blood bath to say, "We told you so."[3]

One service that a media team of trained interviewers (as recommended by Ezell) would do is to deter reporters from being guided—and misguided—by political prejudices and selective perception.

But there are often systematic political and economic sanctions inhibiting journalists' coverage of genocide, state-sponsored massacres, and gross violations of human rights. *Washington Post* columnist Richard Cohen spoke at the conference (his speech is not included here) about the difficulties of getting space for foreign events in U.S. newspapers and the problems reporters face in getting to nongovernmental sources in regions where human rights violations are most apt to occur. Violence, incarceration, and threats against them by state and other political actors and the economic costs of state expulsion of journalists and news bureaus may deter journalists from doing investigative reporting in such places. Thus, there is a large gap between what is possible to do, were there a commitment on the part of the media, and what is likely to be done.

Cohen identified three criteria for a putative genocide to attract the American public: the victims must be seen as innocent, they must have an American constituency, and the United States must be perceived as having some leverage. This brings up the question of how and when the public in the West can be mobilized to prevent genocide, assuming that the West has both potential sanctions and power to do so and a potential constituency driven by conscience and concern for human rights.

Leo Kuper reflects on means of preventing genocide, beginning with recognizing the limits of powerlessness. Human rights petitioners who rely on moral appeals to the powerful to change social struc-

3. William Shawcross, *The Quality of Mercy: Cambodia, Holocaust and Modern Conscience* (New York: Simon and Schuster, 1984), 52–53; see also pp. 54–63.

tures based on discrimination and oppression are and will be generally ineffective. One cannot expect oppressive governments and perpetrators of genocide to change voluntarily.

Focusing on the bystander states, Kuper stresses the failure of the
international community and of individual states to check genocide.
Moral rhetoric cloaks national self-interest and the domination of
"fourth world" nations by third world states. The doctrine of self-
determination "has been domesticated to serve the interests of ruling
classes, most notably in U.N. practice."

Campaigns by nongovernmental human rights organizations can
appeal to a broad constituency, and organizers of campaigns to stop
genocide should try to put together a coalition cross-cutting religious and ethnic groups. This is often difficult as each group tends
to focus on its own trauma. Religious identification and the exten-
siveness of religious discrimination have troubling implications: they
suggest that "religious conditioning contributes at a deeper level to
a general alienation from the victims, facilitating involvement in mass
killings."

International Alert, founded in 1985 by Kuper and others, is an
organization dedicated to preventing the escalation of ethnic conflict
to genocide. Kuper describes his experiences and the group's activities in Uganda, Sri Lanka, and Burundi. He believes that a primary
long-term task is to build a constituency against genocide, "a social
movement comparable to the peace movement . . . [whose] motivation for participation would be predominantly altruistic, in contrast
to the peace movement, which draws on the omnipresent fear of
annihilation in an age of nuclear armaments." Many strategies are
suggested to fit the various types of genocides and the opportunities
they offer for deterrence or intervention.

One underlying problem discussed by both Ervin Staub and David
Matas is how to raise consciousness of genocide and awareness and
empathy with victims. Staub draws on his and others' social-psycho-
logical studies to show how people learn to help others or to become
passive bystanders, relating the outcome to childhood, life experiences, values, and characteristics of the situations in which victims
may be observed. Staub's view of our potential is a dynamic one:

people learn by doing to become more involved and helpful or more passive and detached. Bystanders who remain passive when confronted with the victimization of others themselves change: they devalue the victims further and find justifications for their treatment. We are prone to devalue victims in order to maintain our belief in a "just world"; denying that the victim is innocent affirms that innocent people do not become victims. Just as Cohen suggests, research shows that the bystanders' belief that the victim is innocent is related to their likelihood of helping the victim.

David Matas reflects on the nature of the imperative to remember and learn from the Holocaust. He relates our failure to remember and appreciate the consequences of the disinterest of the United States and Canada in taking in Jewish refugees before and during World War II to our continuing failure to respond to human rights crises. Many have noted how U.S. public opinion surveys showed that a majority of Americans before World War II held the Jews to be wholly or partly responsible for their victimization. This again shows how "just-world" thinking can turn the bystander away from the victim.

Katharine R. Bigelow relates what appears to be a success story in human rights mobilization: how the Bahá'ís outside Iran mobilized public opinion in key states and international organizations against the persecution of Bahá'ís in Iran—convincing people that the Bahá'ís were innocent victims with no political aims against the Islamic Republic of Iran. Iran's policy began with the disaccreditation of Bahá'ís as a legally recognized religion: it was followed by the arrest, disappearance, and execution of the Bahá'í leadership in Iran, the burning and confiscation of Bahá'í houses of worship and the exclusion of Bahá'ís from schools, jobs, and other benefits of Iranian citizens—including, at times, hospitalization and medical attention.

The Bahá'ís of the United States employed a public relations firm to publicize their case and appealed to and testified at hearings of the U.S. Congress, the European Parliament, and U.N. human rights bodies. The persistent protests of these organizations are believed to

have induced Iran to cease jailing and executing the Bahá'ís despite
official Iranian protests rejecting the validity of the appeals. This cessation marks a pattern one might label aborted genocide, but the
Bahá'ís, for tactical reasons, did not.

When prevention has not been undertaken or has failed, we must
consider the punishment of genocide and interventions to stop it.
Vratislav Pechota considers the terms of the UNGC and the possibility of broadening its use by invoking the principle of universal jurisdiction and instituting an international tribunal. Now that the Soviet
Union (which had previously opposed an international criminal court)
is reexamining its policies regarding international protection of human rights, and now that the United States has ratified the convention (in 1988, forty years after its introduction), the time may be
ripe to found such a court to supplement national courts.

Vratislav Pechota suggests that in order to establish universal jurisdiction, the United Nations should create a set of stand-by procedures to indict and try accused perpetrators of genocide: "The
mechanism should be independent, effective, and universal, and it
should be used sparingly." Given the record of the United Nations
in regard to genocide (see Kuper), such a tribunal would be used
very sparingly. Witness the failure of the United Nations to indict
the Khmer Rouge for genocide in Kampuchea.[4]

Hypothetically, there are two risks in detecting cases: (1) over-
looking genocide and (2) falsely labeling rights violations as genocide in order to stigmatize a state. Pechota addresses the latter problem by suggesting safeguards to prevent "the possibility of a group
of states organizing to confer jurisdiction for purposes of propaganda or political embarrassment of other states." The twofold problem suggests the need to combine sociological realism about how
the United Nations and other institutions work with legal drafting
in devising new institutions.

But practical measures that do not demand changes in the UNGC,
Pechota tells us, could be adopted today. These include a specifica-

4. Hannum, "International Law."

tion of the responsibility of countries that border on perpetrators of genocide to signal the act, take evidence, and help victims (only a resolution of the General Assembly is needed), and an international mechanism for the compensation, restitution, and resettlement of victimized groups.

What, one may ask, prevents states from going into other states to check genocide directly? Humanitarian intervention, a doctrine in international law that permits forceful intervention of states to prevent gross violations of the right to life in other states (without their nationals being necessarily involved), has been debated for decades, and there is a body of literature in law and political theory justifying it. There is also much warning that hegemonic states may use humanitarian intervention to mask other motives.

Kuper asserts, however, that intervention is a fact of life, and effective intervenors against genocides are seldom moved by altruistic considerations alone—for example, India in Bangladesh, Tanzania in Uganda, Vietnam in Kampuchea. In two of these cases, intervention ended the killings, but in Uganda they recurred under the succeeding regimes. Kuper, drawing on Bayzler, suggests criteria for humanitarian intervention to prevent its misuse, as does Harff.[5]

But intervention against genocide—and against aggression—is the last resort, often made necessary by the indifference of bystanders and their refusal to sanction the perpetrator. For example, Iraq went into Kuwait after the United States, Britain, France, and the Federal Republic of Germany not only refused to apply sanctions but even helped it rearm after the Iran-Iraq War (including provisions for chemical warfare) in spite of the gassing of the Kurds and continued gross human rights violations. In many other cases, genocidal regimes have instigated wars either through direct aggression or as a result of the consequences of large-scale refugee flight.

As Saeedpour observes, the fact that the recent war against Iraq

5. Barbara Harff, *Genocide and Human Rights: International Legal and Political Issues* (Denver: University of Denver Monograph Series in World Affairs, 1984); see also "Humanitarian Intervention: An Annotated Bibliography," in *Genocide: A Critical Bibliographic Review,* vol. 2, ed. Israel W. Charny (New York: Facts on File, 1991).

was justified by Iraq's violation of another state's territorial integrity reflects the values of states; violation of states is primary, whereas violation of peoples, especially nonstate peoples, is secondary.

Paradoxically, the Gulf War has again demonstrated the linkages between violations. It shows us again that not responding to genocidal massacres tells the perpetrators that they can get away with murder. If this pays off, they are more likely to strike again, as Iraq has done.

The future likelihood of genocides being deterred or checked depends on the answers to several questions. Will the United States and the Soviet Union cooperate to demilitarize conflicts, to encourage negotiation rather than repression, and to create respect for international law? Will policy elites recognize that genocide is a threat to regional and international stability? Will they relate the costs of tolerating genocide to the massive costs of refugee aid, famine relief, and underdevelopment resulting from fear and flight? And finally, will a constituency and a school of social analysts who will demand that governments address these problems emerge?

Part One

DEFINITIONS OF GENOCIDE
AND RESEARCH FINDINGS

Kurt Jonassohn   *Chapter 2*

WHAT IS GENOCIDE?

AUTHOR'S NOTE: I was born in Germany. By pure chance I was able to emigrate early in 1939. My parents and many of my other relatives were not so lucky. Because I had become a refugee and a stranger I naturally turned to sociology—the study of society—as a vocation. Some ten years ago I started to do research on and teach about genocide, together with Frank Chalk, who is a historian. Jointly we established the Montreal Institute for Genocide Studies. Our collaboration has helped us develop a comparative and historical perspective that has resulted in our book *The History and Sociology of Genocide: Analyses and Case Studies* (New Haven: Yale University Press, 1990).

In brief, my own biography has predisposed me to look for an explanation and an understanding of genocide. Even though these may ultimately be beyond reach, my native optimism leads me to continue to search for means of preventing such catastrophes in the future.

From the beginning of our collaboration, Frank Chalk and I have found the definition of genocide contained in the U.N. Convention

I wish to thank Frank Chalk and Helen Fein for their comments on an earlier version of this chapter.

on Genocide, adopted in December 1948, quite unsatisfactory, for one very simple reason: none of the major victim groups of those genocides that have occurred since its adoption falls within its restrictive specifications. This seems to be true regardless of whether we are thinking of Bangladesh or Burundi, Cambodia or Indonesia, East Timor or Ethiopia. The crux of this problem lies in Article II of the U.N. Convention, which limits the term *genocide* to "acts committed with intent to destroy, in whole or in part, a national, ethnical, racial or religious group." Other groups—social, political, economic—do not qualify as victims of genocide because they were omitted from that definition. The reasons for that omission have been discussed by Leo Kuper[1] and are less relevant here than the need for a definition that would cover the planned annihilation of any group, no matter how that group is defined and by whom. Minimally, such a definition should include economic, political, and social groups as potential victims. There have been a number of efforts to amend and expand the U.N. definition of possible victim groups—so far without success.[2]

This lack of success is all the more puzzling since the 1951 U.N. Convention Relating to the Status of Refugees "defines a refugee as any person who, . . . owing to well-founded fear of being persecuted for reasons of race, religion, nationality, membership of a particular social group or political opinion, is outside the country of his or her nationality."[3] These two conflicting definitions, arising from the same organization, seem to produce the paradox that some people fleeing from genocide are recognized as refugees while those unable to flee from the same genocide are not acknowledged as being its victims. So, after many revisions, we have finally adopted the following definition for our own research:

1. Leo Kuper, *Genocide: Its Political Use in the Twentieth Century* (New Haven: Yale University, 1981), ch. 2.
2. Ben Whitaker, *Revised and Updated Report on the Question of the Prevention and Punishment of the Crime of Genocide* (United Nations Economic and Social Council, Commission on Human Rights, E.CN.4. Sub.2, 1985.6: July 2, 1985).
3. Frances D'Souza and Jeff Crisp, *The Refugee Dilemma,* Report no. 43 (London: Minority Rights Group, 1985), 7.

Genocide is a form of one-sided mass killing in which a state or other authority intends to destroy a group, as that group and membership in it are defined by the perpetrator.

The main difference between the U.N. definition and ours is that we have no restrictions on the types of groups to be included. This allows us to include even groups that have no verifiable reality outside the minds of the perpetrators, such as "wreckers" or "enemies of the people"; though such a group may not fall within the usual definition of a group as used in the social sciences, the labeling of a group by the perpetrator suffices to define it. Our definition also allows us to include groups that may be recognized by the social sciences but had previously escaped the imagination of perpetrators, such as the urban dwellers victimized in Pol Pot's Kampuchea.

I must point out, however, that post–World War II cases do not represent the complete range of our interests. On the contrary, we believe we have evidence that genocides have occurred in all parts of the world during all periods of history, from antiquity up to the present day. Our sampling of cases in *The History and Sociology of Genocide* [4] was not meant to be exhaustive, because it is not possible to be expert on all periods of history in all parts of the world. We are convinced that there are cases we are not even aware of, not only because of our own limitations but also because of the "collective denial" that has limited the reporting of cases during most periods of history.

The conference began with a question: what elements do we look for in evaluating situations and events to determine whether we are dealing with a case of genocide? We use three major criteria: (1) there must be evidence, even if only circumstantial, of the intent of the perpetrator; (2) there must be a group whose victimization threatens its survival as a group; and (3) the victimization must be one-sided. We realize that these conditions are problematic; there-

4. Frank Chalk and Kurt Jonassohn, *The History and Sociology of Genocide: Analyses and Case Studies* (New Haven, Conn.: Yale University Press, 1990), pt. 2.

fore we recognize as "genocidal massacres" those events that seem to violate one of our conditions. Let me elaborate.

Of the three criteria, the first one, which requires that there be evidence of intent, is clearly the most difficult to deal with. The Holocaust is the only case in which the perpetrators' leader wrote a book outlining his plans for the state he hoped one day to lead[5] and in which these plans were carried out. Simon Taylor argues convincingly that Adolf Hitler's intention to annihilate the Jews physically was developed and stated publicly well before the Nazis came to power.[6] Not only that; Germany is the only case in which a successor government did not deny that the killings had taken place and agreed to make reparation payments to certain survivors. In most cases of genocide the evidence of intent and planning is difficult to obtain. There are several reasons for this: (1) in many societies such materials are not written down or are destroyed rather than preserved in archives; (2) many perpetrators have recourse to elaborate means of hiding the truth, controlling access to information, and spreading carefully contrived disinformation; and (3) historically, most genocides were not reported because, until the middle of the twentieth century, there appears to have existed a sort of conspiracy of collective denial whereby the disappearance of a people did not seem to require comment or even mention. Just one example: the literature on antiquity is full of the names of peoples, cities, and empires that had disappeared but never mentions what happened to the populations involved. The main exceptions to this secrecy surrounding the most horrendous events in history are certain religiously motivated cases of genocide, whose perpetrators proudly announced their "victories" over the nonbelievers, pagans, or heretics.

So, what can be done to ascertain intent and planning? This apparently formidable problem resolves itself on closer inspection into the problem of obtaining accurate and reliable information about

5. Adolf Hitler, *Mein Kampf* (1924; Boston: Houghton Mifflin, 1971).
6. Simon Taylor, *Prelude to Genocide: Nazi Ideology and the Struggle for Power* (New York: St. Martin's Press, 1985), 218.

killing operations. Once such information has been obtained and verified, it can usually be treated as circumstantial evidence of the intent and planning of the perpetrator. It is not plausible that a group of some considerable size is victimized by man-made means without anyone meaning to do it! This emphasis on intent is important because it removes from consideration in the study of genocides not only natural disasters but also those man-made disasters that took place without explicit planning. Many of the epidemics of communicable diseases that reached genocidal proportions, for example, were caused by unwitting human actions; they could not have been intended because knowledge of the causes of these epidemics was not yet available.

The second criterion for considering a case a genocide is that there must be a group whose victimization threatens its physical survival as a group. There have been many cases in history in which the collective memory, identity, or culture of a group was destroyed without the killing of its members; this is the definition of ethnocide. The fate of many of the indigenous peoples of the Americas illustrates this process. But the threat to the physical survival of the group is essential if genocide is to be distinguished from other death-producing events such as rebellions and civil wars within states and wars between states. Sometimes these lethal events involve massacres, but these should not be considered genocides, for several reasons. Rebellions and civil wars may produce considerable casualties, but they usually do not threaten the survival of either of the opposing groups. In antiquity, wars between states may well have threatened the survival of the losing side because many states were very small. Modern wars have become total wars, however, which is to say that they are no longer combats between opposing military forces but have become conflicts between much larger nation-states involving whole societies. The intent of such warring states is not to annihilate the opposing group but to win the war. In any case, modern nation-states are far too large for total annihilation of the enemy to be achievable. However, some of them have not been above performing an internal genocide during a war if they thought that it might hasten a victory or if they sought to deflect the world's attention from it.

In order for a case to be considered a genocide, a third criterion requires that the victimization be one-sided. This is an essential part of our definition because we mean to exclude from our comparative analyses cases of conflict between more or less equally strong contenders. It also is an additional reason for excluding the casualties of wars between modern nation-states. This does not imply that the victims of genocide must always be weak or defenseless, but it does mean that the perpetrator must be significantly stronger than the victims—otherwise a genocide cannot be carried out at all. Finally, nobody has yet shown that our understanding is enriched by comparing such unlike phenomena as wartime casualties and genocides. The fact that both war and genocide produce massive casualties is a terrible commentary on man's inhumanity to man, but it does not help to understand either phenomenon. We do not believe that there is anything to be gained analytically by comparing cases that have little in common except that they produce large numbers of casualties. There are a great many things that happen in violation of the various U.N. conventions on human rights and our own sense of human dignity and worth; but the causes of such violations will not be better understood by mislabeling them.

Let us turn briefly to the instruments of genocide and how they have changed over time. Perhaps the most obvious observation is that they have often benefited from advances in technology. But it is easy to misinterpret the use of higher technology. Killing very large numbers of people is very hard on those who do the actual work, which includes not only the killing but also the rounding up of victims beforehand and the disposal of the bodies afterward. Modern technology is useful primarily for creating a distance between the killers and the victims. But discipline among the killers seems considerably more important than technology. Thus, even in post–World War II genocides, the most primitive technology is still being used in very poor countries and is obviously still capable of annihilating very large numbers of victims. In both Kampuchea and Burundi, for example, the killers were instructed not to use bullets because they were too costly. And then there is a most horrible invention of ancient vintage, but revived in the twentieth century, that uses a quite primitive technology: the man-made famine. It combines the advantages—for the perpetrators—of costing very little while at the same time putting physical distance between them and the victims. Joseph Stalin used famine in the Ukraine in the early 1930s, and in the 1980s and 1990s it has been used in Ethiopia and in the Sudan.

I wish to expand this excursion into history by commenting briefly on the prevalence of genocide in the ancient and modern worlds and to suggest a tentative explanation of its rise in the twentieth century. Chalk and Jonassohn distinguish two major types of genocides.[7] The first consists of genocides that were practiced in the course of maintaining and expanding empires; they were committed in order to deal with actual or perceived threats, to terrorize real or potential enemies, or to acquire economic wealth. This type of genocide has played a major role in history and seems to have been associated with all empires. The evidence is difficult to gather because it used to be so taken for granted that often neither the perpetrators nor the victims commented on it. The perpetrators included it in their reports of victories and conquests; but either they forgot to mention what happened to the victim populations or their fate was clouded by euphemisms, such as the "razing" of a city—which could mean anything from tearing down its fortified walls to its total destruction, as in Carthage, where the fate of its population is still a matter of debate among specialists. The victims, on the other hand, usually accepted their lot as the fate of the losers. Besides, they did not usually record what had happened to them. The most famous exceptions are the victims of the Mongols under Genghis Khan and his successors; they left voluminous reports on the outrages committed by the conquerors.

Perhaps the easiest way to explain the prevalence of this type of

7. Chalk and Jonassohn, *History and Sociology of Genocide*, pt. 1.

genocide throughout history is to observe that it worked. It did, in fact, eliminate threats, terrorize enemies, and help to acquire economic wealth. It has been on the decline because of the age of empires has passed. Now it occurs only where small indigenous populations control economic resources that more powerful neighbors want to acquire and exploit.

The second type of genocide first occurred in the Middle Ages and was intended to implement a belief, an ideology, or a religion. It has become a paradigmatic type only in the twentieth century. This much can be said simply as a statement of empirical fact. To provide an explanation is much more difficult, in part because most of the relevant research has not yet been done.

Perhaps it is easier to begin by mentioning those explanations with which I disagree, although there will not be space to develop the arguments here. Psychological and psychiatric theories dealing with hostility and aggression are unlikely to be relevant because such drives surely occur among all peoples and because large-scale phenomena such as genocides are not likely to find their explanation in the attributes of individuals. Neither do explanations involving advances in the technology of killing instruments hold much explanatory promise, as already indicated above, although they may be relevant to what some writers have referred to as "omnicide"—that is, a global nuclear war destroying humanity.

More promising approaches would include that of Christina Larner who, encouraged by Norman Cohn, worked out a hypothesis relating the occurrence of genocide to the need of new states and/or regimes to legitimate themselves and to impose a new discipline on a recalcitrant population.[8] This explanation seems plausible enough to warrant further research because both genocides and new regimes and states have become more frequent in the twentieth century. But the research to confirm or deny this hypothesis remains to be done.

Three other arguments should be mentioned briefly. A view most recently expressed by Conor Cruise O'Brien seeks an explanation in

8. Christina Larner, *Enemies of God: The Witch-Hunt in Scotland* (London: Chatto and Windus, 1981), 5.

the rise of nationalism.[9] Hannah Arendt strongly disagrees with this position.[10] Their different interpretations seem in part to hinge on the different ways in which they use the relevant terms. For O'Brien, nationalism is a "terrestrial creed" that encourages glorification of the in-group and devaluation of all out-groups; it has "proved to be the most effective engine for the mobilization of hatred and destruction that the world has ever known." O'Brien holds it responsible for the Holocaust and many other genocides in the modern era. For Hannah Arendt, the nation-states that replaced the earlier empires conferred citizenship rights on everybody; they were tolerant of the minorities within their boundaries; all citizens were equal and their rights were protected by the rule of law. For her, it was not the nation-state or the associated nationalism of its citizens that constituted a threat but, rather, totalitarianism that was lethal; it led to the destruction of the nation-state and to the victimization of its own citizens. Aristide Zolberg has expanded Arendt's analysis to explain the waves of refugees these perpetrator states keep producing. He argues that "the secular transformation of a world of empires . . . into a world of national states" is accompanied by "a generalized political crisis, in the course of which victim groups are especially likely to emerge."[11] What happens to the members of such victim groups depends on the particulars of the situation. They may be discriminated against, expelled, annihilated, or all three.

Larner, O'Brien, Arendt, and Zolberg start out by trying to explain quite different phenomena—from the Great Witch-Hunt to the Holocaust, to the rise of totalitarianism, to the generating of refugee flows—but they arrive at similar explanations. I have mentioned them here because such convergence indicates to me a promising avenue of analysis.

9. Conor Cruise O'Brien, "A Lost Chance to Save the Jews?" *New York Review of Books* 30, no. 7 (April 27, 1989): 27–28, 35.

10. Hannah Arendt, *The Origins of Totalitarianism*, 2d enl. ed. (Cleveland: World Publishing, 1958), 269–290.

11. Aristide R. Zolberg, "The Formation of New States as a Refugee-Generating Process," *Annals of the American Academy of Political and Social Science* 467 (May 1983): 24–38.

As scholars, it is of course very important to us to find a theory that will explain genocide. That would not only satisfy our scientific curiosity but also help us predict its occurrence in the future. As concerned citizens we would find that even more important. But these two desirable aims of theorizing—explanation and prediction—seem to be eluding us. If they are going to be achieved, it apparently will not happen in the near future. That prospect will not discourage scholars, however; they are only too familiar with the need for patience in their scientific efforts. But to the concerned citizen in all of us that daunting prospect should cause us to look for other avenues to prevention. Fortunately, prediction is not a necessary precondition for prevention—a proposition that has not been adequately dealt with in the literature. It is possible to develop a variety of strategies that may help prevent future genocides long before adequate explanations have been found. Thus, our best hope lies in the development and implementation of such strategies.

Barbara Harff   *Chapter 3*

RECOGNIZING GENOCIDES AND POLITICIDES

AUTHOR'S NOTE: When I was a student in my native Germany in the late 1950s, few schools included the Third Reich in their curricula. Although two of my uncles were political prisoners during the late 1930s and early 1940s, they rarely talked about their concentration camp experiences. They did denounce the criminal aspects of the Nazi regime, so that from early childhood I was taught to avoid anyone who had been affiliated in any way with the Nazis. At age sixteen I discovered the horrors of the Holocaust in a book, *Der Gelbe Stern (The Yellow Star),* through its photographs of the survivors, the mass graves, and the extermination facilities.

Currently, I am associate professor of political science at the U.S. Naval Academy. I have written a series of theoretical and empirical articles on the causes and processes of genocide and a monograph, *Genocide and Human Rights: International Legal and Political Issues,* Monograph Series in World Affairs (Denver: University of Denver, 1984). I am now working on a book-length comparative study of victims of the state.

By my definition, genocides and politicides are the promotion and execution of policies by a state or its agents that result in the

deaths of a substantial portion of a group. In genocides the victimized groups are defined primarily in terms of their communal characteristics. In politicides, by contrast, groups are defined primarily
in terms of their political opposition to the regime and dominant
group.

The term *genocide* is fraught with ambiguities, possibly because it
became a catchphrase for the dispossessed. It is often used indiscrim-
inately to describe any and all kinds of social policies and alleged
injuries caused by states; many such acts bear little resemblance to
the crime of genocide as defined in the U.N. Genocide Convention.
The literal meaning refers to the killing of a race or kind (*genos*).
Lemkin coined the term to describe the systematic destruction of
peoples in Europe during the Nazi reign, foremost among them Jews,
Gypsies, and Slavic people.[1]

Genocide, according to Article II of the U.N. Genocide Convention, refers to "acts committed with intent to destroy, in whole or
part, a national, ethnical, racial, or religious group." The article refers to killing members of a group; points c, d, and e specifically refer
to conditions whose cumulative effects are conducive to the destruction of a group. These points are (c) "deliberately inflicting on the
group conditions of life calculated to bring about its physical destruction in whole or in part"; (d) "imposing measures intended to
prevent births within the group"; and (e) "forcibly transferring children of the group to another group." Point b, however, which refers
to acts "causing serious bodily or mental harm to members of the
group," is problematic, for it has given rise to innumerable claims of
victimization. For example, the World Council of Churches made
such a claim on behalf of Australian aborigines during the early 1980s,
at a time when the Australian federal government was making concerted efforts to improve aboriginal welfare. Other claims have referred to acts of repression in which governments disrupted or tried
to destroy the cultural life of a group. In rare cases such acts have led
to isolated massacres, which then became the cause célèbre of belea-

1. Raphael Lemkin, *Axis Rule in Occupied Europe* (Washington, D.C.: Carnegie
Endowment for International Peace, 1944).

guered minorities claiming the advent of a genocide or a holocaust. The exclusion of this problematic point would delimit the crime of genocide to those acts that endanger the *physical* life of group members and thus would eradicate some confusion. Geno/politicides are unfortunately not uncommon, and if we were to extend the usage of the term to all forms of repression that incur death, we would be unable to distinguish between serious and frivolous claims.

I think of genocide as standing in a similar relationship to ecocide (the destruction of the environment) or ethnocide (the destruction of a culture) as premeditated homicide stands to intentional rape. In the case of homicide the perpetrator clearly attempts to destroy the whole person, whereas in the case of rape the objective is to harm, alter, or use the victim. Those who injure the environment or deny groups the ability to propagate their culture are far less likely to plan a genocide than are revolutionaries and despots such as Adolf Hitler, Joseph Stalin, Pol Pot, and Idi Amin—their intentions were obvious. Armed with ideologies that excluded certain groups from the public conscience, these men succeeded in making the victimized groups easy scapegoats.

During the empirical phase of my research, I generated a cross-national data set that identifies episodes of mass murder by governments, and I began to differentiate between genocide and what I identified as politicide. Politicides are events in which the victims are defined primarily in terms of their political position—their class, political beliefs, or organized opposition to the state and the dominant group. In genocides people are defined primarily by their membership in a particular ethnic, religious, national, or racial group. Both are types of extreme state repression, in which coherent policies by a ruling elite result in the deaths of a substantial portion of the targeted group. The difference usually is readily apparent. In genocides the victims share ascriptive traits; in politicides that may or may not be the case. In politicides victims are always engaged in some oppositional activity deemed undesirable by those in power; in genocides that may not be so.

The empirical phase of my research concentrates on cases since

World War II. The rationale for concentrating on post-Holocaust cases is simple. First, I want to show that genocides and politicides are recurrent phenomena. Second, I leave to historians those earlier cases for which empirical evidence is not readily available or for which a substantial literature already exists. But as much as I have tried to avoid the fruitless debate on whether or not the Holocaust was unique and should therefore be treated somewhat differently, it has been impossible to do so, given the comparative nature of my research. Empirical research relies on comparison to explain the origins and consequences of political behavior. All cases have unique properties but also share some discernible patterns with others, from which social scientists can identify some common sequences and outcomes. Evidence shows that the systematic killing of individuals because of their ethnic, religious, or racial traits, or because they share certain political beliefs, has not ceased since 1945. Obviously elites' ability, willingness, and opportunity to kill groups of unwanted people have not disappeared since the Holocaust became part of public memory. If we want to keep alive the memories of all victims of senseless death, we need to recount all of them and identify their killers. We must also develop the ability to monitor ongoing events so that eventually we will be able to forewarn of genocides in the making.

HOW TO DETECT A GENOCIDE

Although "body counts" in principle do not enter the definition of genocide, in practice the destruction of small groups often is not detected until after the fact. As long as one can identify victims as members of a deliberately targeted group whose existence or survival is at stake, numbers of victims are irrelevant. For purposes of identifying cases, however, I count only episodes that last six months, on the ground that it takes time to plan and execute the destruction of a group. Thus, isolated massacres are excluded unless we see some continuity in the form of intermittent but repeated reprisals against such groups; the Iraqi government's treatment of Kurds is a case in

point. But the threshold between massacres and an episode of geno/
politicide is one of inherent uncertainty.

How does one evaluate a situation to determine whether a genocide is in the making? Ideally, all persecuted minority groups or repressed majorities should be monitored on an ongoing basis, but in
practice this is impossible. Thus, we often recognize a situation only
after a number of people are already dead. On the other hand, the
literature abounds with information identifying minorities or majorities that are at risk in various countries. I especially call attention to
the "Minorities at Risk" data set of Ted Robert Gurr, which assesses
the civil and political rights at the societal and national level of 237
minorities in 126 countries.[2] His key indicator of whether an ethnic
or racial group is at risk of human rights violations is the existence
of systematic differential treatment by the larger society. Gurr and I
have published an article comparing forty-four episodes of geno/po-
liticides (see table 3.1) with such groups at risk, which enables us to
identify the groups that are the most probable targets of extreme
repression in the future.[3] Genocides and politicides do not develop
overnight and without warning. We often know that specific coer-
cive violations of rights have taken place.

Sometimes during periods of national emergency basic political
rights are curbed with the intent of protecting rather than punishing
peoples. This can be appropriate in situations in which the victimized groups espouse hate propaganda and are themselves engaged in
violent activities—the Tamil Tigers in Sri Lanka are a case in point.
This is different from situations in which groups have endured officially sanctioned discrimination for some time and then are subjected
to the declaration of a state of emergency, a situation that provides
the climate for further curtailments of rights and abuse. The British-

2. Ted Robert Gurr and James R. Scarritt, "Minorities' Rights at Risk: A Global
Survey," *Human Rights Quarterly* 11 (August 1989): 375–405.
3. Barbara Harff and Ted Robert Gurr, "Victims of the State: Genocides, Politicides and Group Repression since 1945," *International Review of Victimology* 1, no.
1 (1989): 23–41.

Table 3.1: Victims of Genocides and Politicides since World War II[a]

Country	Type, Dates of Episodes[b]	Communal Victims	Political Victims	Numbers of Victims[c]
USSR[d]	P 1943–47		Repatriated Soviet nationals	500–1100
USSR[d]	G 11/43–1/57	Chechens, Ingushi, Karachai, Balkars		230
USSR[d]	G 5/44–1968	Meskhetians, Crimean Tatars		57–175
China	PG 2/47–12/47	Taiwanese nationalists		10–40
USSR[d]	P 10/47–?	Ukrainian nationalists		?
Madagascar	P 4/47–12/48	Malagasy nationalists		10–80
People's Republic of China	P 1950–51		Kuomintang cadre, landlords, rich peasants	800–3000
N. Vietnam	P 1953–54		Catholic landlords, rich and middle peasants	15
Sudan[e]	P 1952–72	Southern nationalists		100–500
Pakistan[e]	PG 1958–74	Baluchi tribesmen		

Country	Type/Date		Target	Number
People's Republic of China	GP 1959		Tibetan Buddhists, landowners	65
Iraq[e]	PG 1959–75		Kurdish nationalists	?
Angola	P 5/61–1962	Kongo	Assimilados	40
Algeria	P 7–12/62		Harkis (French-Muslim troops), OAS supporters	12–60
Paraguay	G 1962–72	Ache Indians		0.9
Rwanda	PG 1963–64		Tutsi ruling class	5–14
Laos	PG 1963–?	Meo tribesmen		18–20
Zaire[f]	P 2/64–1/65	Europeans, missionaries	Educated Congolese	1–10
S. Vietnam	P 1965–72		Civilians in NLF areas	475
Indonesia	GP 10/65–1966	Chinese	Communists	500–1000
Burundi[e]	PG 1965–73		Hutu leaders, peasants	103–205
Nigeria	G 5/10/66	Ibos living in the North		9–30
People's Republic of China	P 5/66–1975		Cultural Revolution victims	400–850

Table 3.1: Victims of Genocides and Politicides since World War II[a] (*Continued*)

Country	Type, Dates of Episodes[b]	Communal Victims	Political Victims	Numbers of Victims[c]
Guatemala	P 1966–84	Indians	Leftists	30–63
India	P 1968–82		Naxalites	1–3
Philippines	PG 1968–85	Moro (Muslim) nationalists		10–100
Equatorial Guinea	GP 3/69–1979	Bubi tribe	Political opponents of Macias	1–50
Uganda	GP 2/71–1979	Karamojong, Acholi, Lango; Catholic clergy	Political opponents of Idi Amin	100–500
Pakistan	PG 3–12/71	Bengali nationalists		1250–3000
Chile	P 9/73–1976		Leftists	2–30
Ethiopia	P 1974–79		Political opposition	30
Kampuchea	GP 1975–79	Muslim Cham	Old regime supporters, urban people, disloyal cadre	800–3000

Indonesia	PG 12/75–present		East Timorese nationalists	60–200
Argentina	P 1976–80		Leftists	9–30
Zaire^e	P 1977–?	Tribal opponents	Political opponents of Mobutu	3–4
Burma	G 1978	Muslims in border region		?
Afghanistan	P 1978–89		Supporters of old regime, rural supporters of rebels	1000
Uganda	GP 1979–1/86	Karamojong, Nilotic tribes, Bagandans	Supporters of Amin regime	50–100
El Salvador	P 1980–present		Leftists	20–70
Iran	GP 1981–?	Kurds, Bahá'ís	Mujahedeen	10–20
Syria	P 4/81–2/82		Muslim Brotherhood	5–25
Sri Lanka	PG 1983–8/87	Tamil nationalists		2–10

Table 3.1: Victims of Genocides and Politicides since World War II[a] (*Continued*)

Country	Type, Dates of Episodes[b]	Communal Victims	Political Victims	Numbers of Victims[c]
Ethiopia	PG 1984–85+		Victims of forced resettlement	?
Somalia	PG 5/88–1989	Issak clan (Northerners)		?

Source: This is an updated version of a table that appeared in the *International Review of Victimology* 1, no. 1 (1989).

a. Episodes of mass murder carried out by or with the complicity of political authorities, directed at distinct communal (ethnic, national, religious, or politically defined groups. Politically organized communal groups, placed in the table between the two column headings, share both kinds of defining traits.

b. This code is based on a more precise categorization of types of genocide and politicide as follows: G = genocide, victims defined communally; P = politicide, victims defined politically; PG = politicides against politically active communal groups; GP = episodes with mixed communal and political victims.

c. Estimates are in thousands. The victims include all civilians reported to have died as a direct consequence of regime action, including victims of starvation, disease, and exposure as well as those executed, massacred, bombed, shelled, or otherwise murdered. Numbers of victims are seldom known with any exactitude, and sometimes no reliable estimates of any kind are available. The numbers shown here represent the ranges in which the best estimates or guesses lie.

d. The first three Soviet episodes all began during and as a consequence of World War II but continued well past the war's end; hence they are regarded as postwar episodes. The second, third, and fourth Soviet episodes all involved the rapid, forced deportation of national groups to remote areas under conditions in which many died of malnourishment, disease, and exposure. Few of these victims were deliberately murdered. The terminal dates for the second and third cases represent the dates on which rights of citizenship were restored to the survivors. Estimates of deaths vary widely, as in most other episodes. Our coding of deaths is based on the more direct and detailed analysis of A. M. Nekrich in *The Punished People: The Deportation and Fate of Soviet Minorities at the End of the Second World War* (New York: W. W. Norton, 1978) rather than the demographic projections of J. G. Dyadkin in *Unnatural Deaths in the U.S.S.R., 1928–1954* (New Brunswick, N.J.: Transaction Books, 1983).

e. These episodes are discontinuous, including two or more distinct periods of mass murder, typically initiated in response to renewed resistance by the victim group.

f. Killings by the short-lived Congolese People's Republic between February 1964 and the recapture of its Stanleyville capital in January 1965.

Malayan treatment of ethnic Chinese in Malaya (1948–1956) may illustrate this point.[4]

An example of a situation that has the potential of developing into a politicide is the practice of tolerating private militias that kill innocent civilians. Such a situation exists at present in the Philippines, where the privileged class and the government are trying simultaneously to preserve the status quo and to fight a Communist insurgency. Militias can easily evolve into killing squads that are not only accepted but often endorsed by governing authorities, as, for example, in El Salvador.

In most conflict analyses participants are assumed to behave rationally. Yet to an outside observer genocide appears irrational. This is especially true of genocides carried out in the service of an ideological doctrine. The annihilation of Jews in Nazi Germany, where even during all-out war the death camps were working to capacity, shows how pure hate can lead to self-defeating behavior. If winning the war was the foremost goal of the Germans, then a well-treated, albeit subjugated, people could have served the war effort by working in war-related jobs. Apparently the foremost goal was the annihilation of European Jewry and the Gypsies and the enslavement of Slavic peoples. Similar irrational policies led to the annihilation of the intelligentsia in Kampuchea in an effort to institute a utopian self-contained peasant society.

How does one begin to explain irrational behavior? In these cases normal standards of behavior cease to have meaning. Does irrational behavior follow some internal logic similar to that of rational behavior? One can start by tracing less bizarre aspects of coercion to the onset of a genocide or politicide. Obviously, the assumption here is that recurrent episodes of discrimination and denial of rights sometimes lead to more severe forms of coercion.

One condition that may predict that genocide is in the making is the practice of denying groups access to political and/or economic positions. In Germany prior to Nazi rule, the Jews were only mar-

4. See Geoffrey Fairbairn, *Revolutionary Guerrilla Warfare: The Countryside Version* (Harmondsworth, Middlesex: Penguin Books, 1974).

ginally integrated politically. Economically Jews were overrepresented in the professions, but traditionally had been excluded from the guilds and civil service. The anti-Semitism that denied Jews access to political office, education, and the professions eroded slowly during the nineteenth century, only to reemerge at the end of the century. Prior discrimination and prejudice made the Jews a convenient target for Nazi ideologues.

In the case of Kampuchea, a tiny elite made up of ethnic Chinese merchants, foreign-educated bureaucrats, and traditional groups surrounding the court enjoyed privileges, although short-lived in the case of the Chinese merchants, which aroused the envy of the peasants. This envy was a pliable tool in the hands of the zealous ideologues of the Khmer Rouge. The Khmer Rouge's early successes in attracting support were a result of foreign intervention, Khmer Rouge's ideology, rampant internal corruption, and widespread poverty, among other factors. Peasant envy of indigenous and minority elites made these groups natural targets for Khmer Rouge fury against all their enemies.

How do we infer that governments deliberately plan and execute genocides or politicides? If the killings are carried out by military or quasi-military groups or death squads, then it follows that decisions to do so have been made at a high level. Unfortunately many people may die before we can decide whether this is a genocide. Even more difficult is the case of civil war, in which there is no effective central authority. Who is responsible for the killings? Pogroms, however, are distinct from genocides: they are short-lived outbursts by mobs, which, although often condoned by authorities, rarely persist.

What other factors distinguish genocide from lesser forms of repression? Genocidal policies require planning and preparation. Therefore we should look for evidence of official deliberations in which comprehensive plans are laid for controlling/relocating/eliminating categories of people. Similarly, the early stages of genocidal policies are likely to include campaigns of hate propaganda and the issuance of directives and laws that provide justifications and instructions for acting against target groups. Intermediate phases may include campaigns of deception during which a resistant public is lulled by an apparent let-up in persecution or by official denials of wrong-doing. During the implementation phase, the institution of new agencies or bureaucracies may give us a clue about what to expect. The final phase frequently includes a systematization of ongoing forms of persecution, which we may be able to observe by tracing the establishment of special forces, the fortification of labor camps, and an increased emphasis not on the final objective (killing people) but on the means of destruction. An example is the Wannsee conference in Nazi Germany on January 20, 1942, which systematized Nazi policies of extermination that were already well underway: it accelerated the construction of new facilities and the fortification of former labor camps into full-fledged extermination centers and routinized the mass deportation of Jews from the occupied states of Europe.

Evidence suggests that the type and organization of a government also play a role in determining the scale of a genocide. Democracies are the least likely to use systematic repression; totalitarian and authoritarian governments are the most likely to do so. But regardless of the political form, bureaucratically developed structures are best equipped to execute a genocide on the scale and in the manner of the Holocaust.

DEATH IN WAR AND GENOCIDE: THE MEANS AND ENDS OF DESTRUCTION

During war civilians get killed, sometimes by the thousands. How do we differentiate between a genocide and deaths incidental to combat? International wars are fought between states, whereas perpetrators of genocide rarely cross boundaries unless they occupy other countries. Most civilized states adhere to the rules of war, which proscribe the intentional killing of civilians during war. These principles rarely are applied fully, but the intent nonetheless is to avoid killing noncombatants.

During a nuclear war, the distinction between combat soldiers and civilians becomes irrelevant. The nature of total warfare changes the equation. Most nuclear strategists stress the irrationality of total war because it ensures mutually assured destruction. Few are willing to admit that nuclear weapons will ever be used in a "limited" war. Yet, strategies designed to knock out the opponent's nuclear arsenal may make massive civilian casualties unavoidable. Thus, some scholars see total war as a genocide because it is likely to result in the annihilation of a large percentage of the world's population. Nevertheless, nuclear war is not genocide. Whether or not nuclear strikes are genocidal depends on the intent of those who order them. Limited and defensive uses of nuclear weapons are not inherently genocidal, even if they have the unwanted consequences of massive civilian deaths. This is not to say, however, that genocides cannot take place during a war.

Another type of war in which many civilian members of a specific national group are likely to be killed is guerrilla war. What are the differences between civilian victims of such a war and victims of genocide? Let's examine a worst-case scenario: a village woman carrying a child conceals a hand grenade, which she throws in the midst of a group of soldiers. Three are killed, and the woman and child are shot on the spot. If the officer in charge now orders the whole village demolished and the villagers killed, this is a massacre, a war crime. If such excesses become a regular occurrence with superiors doing little to prevent them, we have a case of criminal war: war crimes are committed and tolerated with regularity. If, however, the authorities order the killing of a whole group or class of people in a larger area because some of them are suspected of resistance, we have a genocide or politicide. In other words, we need to know who is killed, by whom, and with what intent. An example is the 1904–1906 genocide against the Hereros in southwest Africa. The German commander, Lothar von Trotha, said, to justify reprisals, "The nation as such must be annihilated or if this is not possible from a military standpoint, then they must be driven from the land."[5] Seldom do we

5. Jon M. Bridgman, *The Revolt of the Hereros* (Berkeley and Los Angeles: University of California Press, 1981), 128.

have such clear-cut declarations of the intentions of perpetrators, but often there are other telling clues about their objective.

Such scenarios have been played out repeatedly in situations of guerrilla and revolutionary wars as well as by occupying forces in interstate wars. It is even more difficult to make distinctions in cases of civil war where there is no effective central authority, responsibility for order is in the hands of warring factions, and civilians are killed routinely as a strategy to weaken the opponent. Here we have to look closely at the speeches and declarations of those in charge of each faction to assess intent.

Finally, we need to consider the means by which a genocide is implemented. Have the means changed since enlightened people embarked upon efforts to break down the barriers of ignorance and prejudice? The lesson of the Holocaust tells a different story: medieval torture methods coexisted with the techno-death of millions. Unfortunately, neither the Holocaust nor the active efforts of international agencies—private and public—have eliminated extreme brutality, though they seem to have banished it to the fringes of the third world. Kampuchea is a case in point. I interviewed refugees in Thailand in 1981, who told me abhorrent tales of mayhem and murder with clubs and knives and of children ordered to kill their parents. The worst cases are little different from the barbarism of Timur Lenk, whose mountains of skulls were the legacy of a pillaging conqueror. Today's perpetrators are more likely to burn or bury the dead. Is it because they realize that they have committed a crime against humanity?

RECOGNITION, DENIAL, AND LABELING OF CASES

Part Two

ORGANIZATION, DENIAL
AND LABELING OF CASES

Bill Frelick   *Chapter 4*

REFUGEES: CONTEMPORARY
WITNESSES TO GENOCIDE

AUTHOR'S NOTE: I am a senior policy analyst with the U.S. Committee for Refugees and associate editor of the *World Refugee Survey*. My work has brought me into contact with refugee victims of human rights abuse from many lands. Most recently, I interviewed Central American refugees and asylum seekers in Mexico and wrote *Running the Gauntlet: The Central American Journey through Mexico*, published by the U.S. Committee for Refugees, Washington, D.C., in January 1991.

Articles I have written on genocide include "Teaching about Genocide as a Contemporary Problem" in the September 1985 *Social Education;* "Iran's Bahá'ís: Victims of Continuing Genocide" in the *Christian Century* of December 3, 1986; "Iranian Bahá'ís and Genocide Early Warning" in the fall 1987 *Social Science Record;* and "Refugees: A Barometer of Genocide" in the *World Refugee Survey: 1988 in Review.*

An essay on Cambodian genocide recently published in the *Human Rights Quarterly* begins: "The atrocities that occurred in Democratic Kampuchea under the rule of Pol Pot and the Khmer Rouge from 1975 to 1979 were, at first, dismissed as only the rumors of refugees. Early reports of widespread killings often were rejected as exaggerated or anticommunist diatribes."[1] How can we better assess refugee testimonials so that true accounts of genocide are not again so easily dismissed? This chapter will focus on the testimony of refugees as one of the indicators of whether genocide is occurring in their homelands. I will also discuss how interviewers can best elicit true accounts from refugees and suggest ways of establishing corroborating evidence in the absence of direct access to the areas generating refugee flows.

The essay will first examine the situations of three refugee groups who fled their homelands in 1988—the Dinkas, Kurds, and Hutus. Each emerged from relative obscurity onto the world stage at least briefly in 1988 as a result of its members falling victim to atrocities at the hands of the armed forces or elements allied with the governments of the Sudan, Iraq, and Burundi, respectively. The actual number of victims will never be known, but it is certain that thousands, even hundreds of thousands, of their number were killed or died as a result of violence directed against them. Many thousands more have fled or have been trapped while attempting to flee to the safety of neighboring countries or, in the case of the Dinkas, to safer areas within their own country.

Detecting genocide as a contemporary event is not a matter of analyzing historical archives but rather rests on finding living witnesses, determining the truth of their testimonies, and deciding whether those testimonies fit a pattern of persecution or demonstrate a genocidal intent—the wish to destroy, in whole or in part, the group in question.

Being able to detect genocide as it is occurring, and to name it as such, gives us at least the possibility of intervening to prevent these horrors from worsening. From the point of view of preventing genocide—or at least curbing it—as an ongoing occurrence, we need not only to seek the truth but also to search for ways to break through

1. Hurst Hannum, "International Law and Cambodian Genocide: The Sounds of Silence," *Human Rights Quarterly* 11, no. 1 (February 1989).

the barriers to belief. People seem especially reluctant to see genocide as a contemporary reality. It is something long ago or far away, perhaps even sui generis, as the Holocaust is sometimes framed. Our tendency, it seems, is to search for a reason *not* to believe.

The absence of objective on-the-scene observers to record actual killings always provides room for doubt. We wait for "objective facts" before being moved to respond. To establish that the problem is genocide, each incident must be documented, each killing stand as a separate fact, and then these discrete facts must be understood as a totality fitting into a pattern of intent on the part of the persecutors to destroy a national, ethnic, racial, or religious group. We are understandably reluctant to use the term *genocide* lightly. We do not want to cheapen its meaning to those who have been its victims. On the other hand, given that no one committing genocide is going to allow neutral witnesses to record it, are we necessarily taking the use of the term out of the hands of those in the contemporary political arena, who could work to stop massive human rights violations, and consigning it only to the rarified world of the historian?

At what point can a contemporary observer accurately show that persecution has become genocide? Was that point reached in 1988 in the cases of Sudan, Burundi, and Iraq? How does one establish the truth of "facts" in the absence of direct observation and documentation?

ESTABLISHING INTENT

The intent of the perpetrator of genocide is often as difficult to establish as is the act itself. Yet, at least in terms of the U.N. Convention on the Prevention and Punishment of the Crime of Genocide, the charge of genocide has meaning only when there is an established intent to destroy, in whole or in part, the group in question. Rarely is the intent so clearly articulated as when Hujjatu'l-Islam Qazai, president of the revolutionary court in Shiraz, Iran, justified the destruction of Iran's Bahá'í community by declaring:

The Iranian nation has determined to establish the government of God on earth. Therefore, it cannot tolerate the perverted Bahá'ís who are instruments of Satan and the followers of the devil and of the super powers and their agents. . . . It is absolutely certain that in the Islamic Republic of Iran there is no place for Bahá'ís and Bahá'ísm. . . . Before it is too late the Bahá'ís should recant Bahá'ísm, which is condemned by reason and logic. Otherwise, the day will soon come when the Islamic nation will deal with them in accordance with its religious obligations, as it has dealt with other hypocrites. . . . The Muslim nation will, God willing, fulfill the prayer of Noah [from the Koran]: "And Noah said, Lord, leave not a single family of Infidels on the Earth: For if thou leave them, they will beguile thy servants and will beget only sinners, infidels."[2]

On the contrary, the usual practice is for governments engaged in massive repression to minimize the situation, to deny the worst allegations, or even to declare amnesties and say that normalcy has been restored. Typical of this response was an interview on September 9, 1988, with President Saddam Hussein of Iraq:

This is what is happening. A group of collaborators was used by Iran along with its occupation army to harm Iraq's military efforts in northern Iraq. When the Iranian Army was expelled from the borders, naturally this group of collaborators lost any military might that would make it capable of confronting our Army. Therefore, it collapsed. And when our Army advanced toward the Turkish borders to purge areas there of their remnants, they used threats to intimidate some villagers, telling them that the Iraqi Army would allegedly think of them as outlaws. However, there is nothing in the history of the Iraqi Army even in the worst cases in which it harmed a child, a woman, or an old man or perpetrated a similar practice. Some of these village residents escaped or entered Turkish territory under the duress of the saboteurs, who sought to use them to protect themselves from any Army strikes, considering that they have children and women and also for other motives.

2. Interview with Hujjatu'l-Islam Qazai, in *Khabar-i-Junub*, February 22, 1983. Full text reprinted in Persian and translated into English in *Major Developments in the Situation of the Bahá'í Religious Minority in Iran: July 1982–July 1983: A Report on the Persecution of a Religious Minority* (New York: Bahá'í International Community, U.N. Office, 1983), 27–28.

Hence, after Iraq had affirmed its strength and capability, it announced an amnesty that even included the sabotage leaders. I think that you heard of the amnesty. It is a complete and comprehensive amnesty, which is to be enjoyed by all except one man.[3]

According to Saddam Hussein's version, the Kurds fled under duress from threats and intimidation from saboteurs and collaborators. No mention is made of destroyed villages or of chemical attacks; and although he admits that the army advanced toward the border, he does not acknowledge that the Iraqi military even engaged them in hostilities. There certainly is no expressed intent to destroy the Kurds. In fact, he extends an amnesty to those who have fled.

Intent is difficult enough to pin down when the perpetrators are silent; it becomes more difficult when they are engaged in sophisticated denials. In such cases, the pattern of abuse is an important factor to consider. President Hussein's assertion that "there is nothing in the history of the Iraqi Army even in the worst cases in which it harmed a child, a woman, or an old man" is readily contradicted by the photos of Halabja following the chemical attack in May. But a historical pattern is apparent as well. In the summer of 1987, reports circulated that about one hundred Kurdish villages had been destroyed by bombing and chemical weapons and that their inhabitants—12,500 families by some accounts—had been forced into resettlement camps in the southern, non-Kurdish region. The remains of vacated villages reportedly were dynamited and bulldozed. These accounts of mass destruction and displacement in 1987 and 1988 are consistent with Kurdish reports of the Iraqi response to the aborted Kurdish uprising of 1974 and the events following the withdrawal of Iranian forces after an earlier incursion in 1983. The more recent accounts differ only in the allegation that chemical weapons were used against the civilian population.

Patterns of persecution are important in establishing intent. Es-

3. Interview with President Saddam Hussein, Iraqi News Agency, reprinted by Foreign Broadcast Information Service, in *Daily Report: Near East and South Asia*, September 9, 1988, 36.

pecially in the absence of stated objectives, these patterns provide a basis for drawing inferences about the intentions of those committing widespread abuses. That the massacres of Kurds, Dinkas, and Hutus in 1988 were not isolated occurrences lends credence to our worst fears. In 1972, some 100,000 Hutus were massacred in Burundi, killings that targeted Hutu leadership and decimated a generation of educated young men. As mentioned above, several crackdowns on Iraq's Kurdish minority have occurred in recent decades. In 1975, after American-supplied arms to the Kurds were abruptly shut off by the shah of Iran, the Iraqis were able to crack down on the Kurds with impunity, and hundreds of villages were destroyed in an effort to scatter the Kurds and prevent them from consolidating political power. In Sudan, the Arabized northerners have for centuries attempted to dominate the African southerners, including the Dinka, who have traditionally been targeted for abduction and sold into slavery. After independence in 1955, a brutal civil war ensued in which several hundred thousand people are estimated to have been killed and a million southerners forced to flee the country. Large numbers of southerners were massacred, tortured, or imprisoned. The renewal of civil war in recent years follows the earlier pattern: Khartoum has exploited centuries-old traditional ethnic rivalries by arming other "African" ethnic groups—the Mundari, the Nuer, and the Fertit—who not only have killed thousands of Dinkas outright but have looted and stolen the cattle that are the backbone of the Dinkas' pastoral economy, destroyed crops, prevented new crops from being planted, and attacked food convoys. Also armed have been Arabized groups, such as the Rizeigat, who have perpetrated massacres against the Dinkas and renewed the practice of abducting Dinka children and selling them into slavery.

As repression and violence escalated again in 1988, all three governments prevented international observers from entering their countries to investigate the allegations of widespread, systematic murder. The Sudanese government in Khartoum threatened to eject international humanitarian agencies operating in the north if they ventured into the south. Blocking relief efforts achieved the dual objective of destroying the Dinkas by starvation and concealing this practice from the outside world. Calling the massacres an "internal problem," Burundi's president, Maj. Pierre Buyoya, categorically rejected any internationally supervised investigation.[4] Similarly, Iraq said it would not allow a U.N. team to investigate allegations that its government had used chemical weapons against the Kurdish population, saying, "This is an Iraqi issue, a domestic issue, not an international one."[5] But Iraq took a more sophisticated approach than mere stonewalling. It attempted to whitewash its activities by flying journalists via helicopter over areas where calm seemed to prevail. By controlling access, it attempted to limit news reporting to the story it wanted told. But reporters in this instance saw through the attempt to manipulate the news. They discovered that the Kurds who were presented to them for interviews—supposedly returned Kurdish refugees who had accepted Hussein's amnesty offer—had in fact never left the country. They also chanced to see a truckload of Iraqi soldiers on the tarmac wearing gas masks.[6]

Saddam Hussein and other contemporary leaders are not alone in denying that massive human rights violations are taking place within the borders of their countries. When the Indonesians killed an estimated 10 to 30 percent of the population of East Timor in the mid-1970s, they were careful to keep the doors closed. To this day, Turkey denies slaughtering more than a million Armenians at the turn of the century. The full extent of other large-scale massacres, such as the one that destroyed the kulaks in the Soviet Union in the time of Joseph Stalin, are only now beginning to be known.

THE FAILURE TO RESPOND

Ironically, the largest crimes often seem to garner the least attention. Relative to the scale of the atrocities they have committed, the mass-

4. "President Rules Out Inquiry," Bujumbura Domestic Service, reprinted by Foreign Broadcast Information Service, in *Daily Report: Sub-Saharan Africa,* August 30, 1988, 2.

5. Interview with Ambassador Abdul-Amir al-Anbari, in "Envoy Says Iraq Will Reject Demands for a U.N. Inquiry," *Washington Post,* September 14, 1988, Al, A16.

6. Patrick E. Tyler, "Kurds Disappoint Iraqi PR Effort," *Washington Post,* September 18, 1988.

killing machines of this century have been remarkably successful at keeping their crimes hidden or at least obscured. How the Nazi extermination camps remained out of the public eye continues to be a subject of painful debate and reflection. Escapees testified to horrors being committed, but too often people refused to listen to them.

Even now when word seeps out through refugees that genocide is occurring, the world is slow to believe. When the Khmer Rouge controlled Cambodia, journalists stationed across the border in Thailand interviewed refugee survivors of the ongoing holocaust. At the time, however, their reports were dismissed as exaggerated: some said that refugee testimonials are unreliable and impossible to corroborate. By the time Pol Pot was driven into the hills and the Vietnamese saw it as in their interest to open the killing fields to the outside world, it was too late.

Many reasons have been suggested for our disbelief or failure to respond. Perhaps we are inured to tales of third world suffering—starvation in Biafra yesterday; flooding and disease in Bangladesh today. And if we believe the accounts of mass atrocities, we simply do not react to them. We seem unable to accommodate the world's suffering, especially if we believe that nothing we feel or do will make a difference.

Perhaps our ethnocentrism limits our concern to our own kind, members of our own race, religion, nationality. When a toddler was trapped in a well in Texas not too long ago, Americans shared the anguish of her parents and tuned in hourly to find out whether she had been rescued. But, objectively speaking, how did that accident involving a single child compare to the horrors being deliberately and systematically committed against hundreds of thousands of children elsewhere?

Perhaps it is the sheer numbers involved in genocide (literally, the murder of a race or a people) that keep us from responding. The murder of 6 million Jews by the Nazis can become an abstraction because our minds cannot fathom 6 million individual persons, each with his or her own identity. But numbers do, at the least, establish scale. And the scale of atrocity makes an impact on our consciousness even as we grapple to come to terms with individual realities. Part of the credibility of refugee testimony is established not by anything that is said but by the fact of mass exodus itself. Refugees truly "vote with their feet." When more than fifty thousand Kurds cross into Turkey in a sudden influx, especially when flight was not typical of responses to previous crackdowns by the Iraqi regime, the numbers alone underscore the testimonials. The same can be said for the more than fifty thousand Hutus who fled into Rwanda, or the more than eighty thousand refugees, the vast majority of them Dinkas, who fled into Ethiopia in 1988.

In 1985, William Stanley, a statistician, used multivariate regression analysis to show a close correlation between refugee flows out of El Salvador and political violence in that country.[7] What Stanley found in the case of El Salvador could be replicated many times over. In many cases, refugees are the measure of genocide in the making, a barometer of repression that provides warning that something so dangerous is happening as to impel people to flee their homes and country. They are an especially valuable indicator in the absence of neutral observers to record the human rights situation within their countries. It doesn't take a statistician to tell us that 3 million Afghan refugees in Pakistan and another 2 million in Iran mean that something is seriously wrong in Afghanistan.

But, as Arthur Koestler once commented, "Statistics don't bleed."[8] The numbers tell a story. They can be compelling. But they tell only the broad outlines of the story. Moreover, a focus on numbers alone can be misleading. A mass exodus is a good indication that a serious problem exists, but the absence of a mass exodus does not necessarily mean that genocide is not occurring. In some of the worst genocidal situations—the Holocaust is the prime example—the determination to destroy the victim group is so strong that routes of escape are blocked and refugee flows prevented.

7. William Stanley, "Statistical Evidence Indicates Many Salvadorans in U.S. Flee from Violence," *Refugee Reports* 6, no. 8 (August 16, 1985).

8. Arthur Koestler, quoted by Samuel Totten, "The Personal Face of Genocide: Words of Witnesses in the Classroom," *Social Science Record* 24, no. 2 (Fall 1987).

REFUGEE TESTIMONIALS

Whether the refugee numbers are large or small, the refugee testimonials provide vital information about ongoing genocide. Political reality is such that the final analysis of their accuracy must be left to the historians. But there are factors to consider in assessing their credibility that need not wait for the historian's judgment. In practical terms, the credibility of the refugee rests largely on the credibility of the interviewer and on the circumstances of the interview. If interviews are conducted in the presence of a group, for example, they are likely to result in a group consensus, not an individual account about the experiences that led the refugee to flee. In the presence of a group of compatriots, a refugee is less likely to contradict what others in the group are saying. The tendency, rather, will be to corroborate each other's stories.

Testimonials are more likely to be accurate the more recently the refugees have arrived from their homeland. Refugees who have been in camps for longer periods of time are more likely to succumb to the temptation to mythologize or exaggerate experiences to suit the psychological and political needs of life in exile. The inclusion of legendary elements in a refugee account is not unlike what happens with other oral histories generally and does not discredit the testimony as a whole. The worth of the testimony is rarely based on its face value, but on how it stands up when evaluated, when tested for internal consistency and corroboration with other testimonies or outside "facts," and when firsthand observations are distinguished from inferences and accounts based on secondary sources. In any case, recent arrivals are more likely to recount their experiences straightforwardly as discrete experiences without attempting to filter them through their own interpretations or to resolve what may seem to them to be contradictions.

Refugees tend to be fearful. They have often experienced trauma in their home country and feel acute uncertainty about their fate in the country of asylum. The interviewer needs to be aware that the refugee is a survivor and is still trying to survive even as the interview is taking place. This can result either in understating the situation in the home country for fear that the testimony might somehow be leaked back home or in overstating the situation out of the refugee's desire to "pass the test" and be allowed to stay or be considered for resettlement in a third country. The refugee might try to anticipate what he thinks the interviewer wants to hear and answer accordingly. Interviews of refugees often do take place in the context of their being screened for refugee status. Or they can be conducted by journalists who might not take adequate care to ensure that testimonies are taken individually and are corroborated.

Given the circumstances in which refugee interviews are likely to take place, it is essential to try to establish trust between the interviewer and the refugee. At the minimum, this means that interviews should be conducted individually and assurances given that confidentiality will be respected. Cultural sensitivity, fluency in language (or competent translators), and specific questions all contribute to the value of the interview. If the refugee is suspicious of the translator, the interview will never get off the ground. Particular care should be taken to choose translators who are working in politically neutral roles, such as health care workers or persons affiliated with relief or religious organizations. They should speak the native language of the refugee, not simply another language the refugee might understand. Tape recordings of the interviews are valuable not only for a complete historical record but also for a later check on the accuracy of translations in the field.

It is helpful to start the interview by asking about the family before the refugee-causing situation began, both to establish trust and rapport with the refugee by showing concern about his or her life and situation and to provide a baseline for comparison to the time when the situation deteriorated. It also keeps the refugee narrowly focused on his or her own experiences and observations. During the course of the interview, the same key questions should be asked in several different contexts to provide an internal check on accuracy.

The interviewer also needs to be aware of the level of sophistication of the refugee being interviewed. An educated refugee leader might be more articulate than his cohorts, but not necessarily more accurate in recounting the situation in the homeland. An illiterate refugee, on the other hand, can often provide extremely important information but might be vague about numbers or the dates when incidents occurred. Such refugees might profitably be encouraged to draw pictures to diagram key experiences or to track events by seasonal agricultural cycles.

Every effort needs to be made to understand the culture of the refugees and to encourage them to communicate their experiences as fully, but as comfortably, as possible. Interviews of refugee women are often the most challenging and difficult, as the traumatic experiences they have encountered often involve sexual assault or other sensitive and personal matters considered to be taboo subjects of discussion, particularly with a male. Yet, especially if interviewed by a woman, female refugees often provide fresh and important insights overlooked by their male companions. Male members of an interview team can act as a lightning rod for officials, refugee leaders, and others inclined to talk about politics and similar matters, and female interviewers are frequently able to talk privately and in detail about the refugee experience.

In addition to the quality of the interviews, the quantity can be an important factor in determining the situation in the home country. More interviews make it possible to establish contradictions and concurrences. The more witnesses independently interviewed on a given episode, the more accurately it can be reconstructed. In addition, at least some random samples in the interviewing process can help ensure a cross section of accounts. At the same time, it is useful within the random sample to interview family units who have shared the same experiences and whose accounts can be cross-checked.

Whenever possible, refugees should be interviewed in different locations. Sometimes the distance between camps or difficulties in communication from one refugee settlement to another permit the interviewer to cross-check refugee accounts. If a testimonial in one camp can be corroborated by refugees in other locations, especially when the opportunity to communicate between camps is remote, the credibility of the testimony is greatly enhanced. It is also helpful to interview refugees who have arrived from different locations within the home country.

Other objective measures of refugee conditions can play a critical role in determining whether genocide is occurring. Medical evidence about the condition of the refugees is essential. It was all the more frustrating in the case of the 1988 Kurdish exodus that Turkey, which had its own reasons for minimizing the Kurdish situation, did not give international medical personnel adequate access to the refugees. Medical evidence is particularly useful when it goes beyond the anecdotal and takes on epidemiological significance. For example, could we have determined a pattern of chemical weapons–induced sequelae among Kurdish refugees from certain towns or provinces? Could a pattern of mortality have been discerned among Sudanese refugees that would have shown disproportionate starvation or evidence of malnutrition among the Dinkas as opposed to other ethnic groups fleeing the same areas? Could we have determined that the wounds inflicted on Hutu survivors were the result of bayonets, available only to the army, thus establishing its responsibility for the massacres?

The evidence based on the refugees themselves—medical, testimonial, demographic—should be compared with whatever other sources may be available on human rights conditions in the homeland. Perhaps sources internal to the regime have leaked information documenting atrocities or the intent behind them. The accounts of defectors, though subject to rigorous tests for credibility, can reveal the internal dynamics of genocidal campaigns. Other evidence may be available from sources within the country who nevertheless remain independent of the regime, such as journalists, diplomats, or nongovernmental organizations.

THE HUMAN FACE OF GENOCIDE

Although the particular individual perspective of survivors may make it difficult for them to tell their story in all its complexity and with objective accuracy—as no doubt occurred in the yellow-rain sagas of Hmong refugees fleeing from Laos[9]—the refugee accounts nevertheless provide not only the bare-bones facts, not only the eyewitness testimony we need to determine what really happened. They also provide a human face, which conveys the reality of genocide. If we are to do anything with this information, if we are to stop genocide at the time it is occurring, the information needs to break through the barriers of disbelief and apathy.

The impact of genocide becomes real the moment homicide becomes reality. We can better comprehend one murder than the murder of thousands. The Nazi Holocaust becomes real to us through the person of Anne Frank. One cannot read her words without mourning her death. Only when we mourn a single victim can we begin to comprehend the enormity of the crime.

Refugees are the living Anne Franks. They call for our response. The bayonet wounds on the legs and backs of Hutu women and children, the scarred and blistered skin of Kurdish refugees, the emaciated bodies of starving Dinkas—these tell us most clearly that lives are in danger. The fact of their flight itself testifies to that, and their words can and should be weighed in determining the situation they have fled. When this evidence is striking, and when it fits into a pattern of conduct toward the refugee groups in question such that intent to destroy them can be reasonably inferred, then the situation is well-enough established to invoke the word *genocide* as at least a threatened occurrence. We may discover that though horrible human rights abuses have occurred, they do not add up to genocide; the aftermath of the massacre of Hutus in Burundi suggests that this might be the case—the government moved to stem the violence, and most of the refugees who fled into Rwanda returned. But in other cases, the weight of the evidence moves in the other direction. We certainly should not use the term lightly. But if we are serious about preventing genocide, we should not shy away from talking about its threat in specific ongoing situations that warrant an extraordinary humanitarian response.

9. Julian Robinson, Jeanne Guillemin, and Matthew Meselson, "Yellow Rain: The Story Collapses," *Foreign Policy* 68 (Fall 1987).

Vera Beaudin Saeedpour   *Chapter 5*

ESTABLISHING STATE MOTIVES
FOR GENOCIDE: IRAQ AND
THE KURDS

AUTHOR'S NOTE: After marrying a Kurd from Iran, I discovered that the
Oxford English Dictionary defined *Kurd* as "one of a tall, pastoral and predatory people." I subsequently found that both the *Random House* and *Scrib-
ner's* dictionaries characterized the Kurds as "warlike." In the course of my
research to support revisions, I became convinced that unless attention could
be drawn to the Kurdish plight, the Kurds would be prime candidates for
cultural and physical annihilation.

In 1981 when I established the Kurdish Program, it was the first American organization devoted to focusing attention on the plight of the Kurds
of the Middle East. At that time they were the fourth largest ethnic group
in the region. Currently, with a total population of more than 25 million,
they rank third behind the Arabs and the Turks. Yet even the existence of so
large a Kurdish population was virtually unknown to the American public.
Five years later when the program opened the Kurdish Library, the only
institution of its kind in the Western Hemisphere, still only a handful of

Americans outside academe, human rights, and government had any knowledge of Kurdish issues.

It was only with Iraq's chemical attacks against Halabja in March 1988 that the plight of the Kurds drew international press coverage. Unfortunately, even then, despite worldwide revulsion and rhetorical condemnation, neither the United States nor the United Nations acted. Official reluctance to impose sanctions against the Iraqi regime gave Saddam Hussein the green light to again deploy chemical weapons on a larger scale against the Kurds little more than five months later.

That there should have followed in January 1991 war against the Iraqi regime justified by its violation of territorial integrity clearly indicates the priorities of nations. Until the priorities of the international community are reordered to place human life in a loftier position, I fear that our efforts will be largely relegated to recording atrocities in history books.

Chemical weapons attacks against Kurdish civilian populations in 1988 have been widely interpreted as retributive actions by the Iraqi government against an unassimilated minority engaged in armed insurgency allied with Iran in the recent Iran-Iraq War. For example, the *Washington Times* of September 9, 1988, quoted this statement from Amnesty International's London headquarters: "The mass killings are part of a systematic and deliberate policy by the Iraqi government to eliminate large numbers of Kurds . . . as a punishment for their imputed political sympathies and in retaliation for the activities of opposition Kurdish forces." And this from the *New York Times* of September 5, 1988: "In Iraqi eyes, their [the Kurds'] sin has been to form a fifth column in the war with Iran, taking support from Teheran in their campaign for far greater autonomy than Baghdad has already granted them. The campaign in northern Iraq, diplomats in Baghdad said recently, is to avenge that role."

This essay argues that the poison gas attacks in August 1988 cannot be explained simply as a response to Kurdish rebellion or the Kurds' role in the Iran-Iraq War but are better explained as the final phase of a deliberate Iraqi plan to remove Kurds permanently from their ancestral lands for economic and strategic reasons. It suggests the need to examine both the geographical pattern of the attacks and state aims—which often tend to be confused with state justifications.

The accompanying map, prepared by the Kurdish Library, was redrawn from a map contained in a September 21, 1988, Senate Foreign Relations Committee staff report identifying the sites of the chemical attacks that occurred in the final week of August.[1] Targeted sites are underlined. What the map reveals—and what has largely been overlooked in analyses of the events of August—is what may well have been the primary motive behind Iraq's choice of this particular region of Iraqi Kurdistan for a major chemical offensive. Note that the targeted sites fall predominantly within a triangle bounded by the Kurdish cities of Dihuk, Zakho, and Amadiya. Traversing and immediately to the south of the triangle are three facilities of primary importance to Iraq: a major highway running through Dihuk and Zakho into Turkey and connecting into Europe; a major railway reaching across the border of Syria; and the Iraqi-Turkish oil pipeline. The map graphically supports the thesis that the Iraqi offensive in August 1988 served to remove this segment of Iraq's indigenous Kurdish population from proximity to these facilities.

Viewed in historical perspective, this move constituted the final phase of an Iraqi policy initiated more than a quarter century ago to bring an end to periodic Kurdish insurrections aimed at achieving some sort of parity with the ruling Arabs. In 1963, following the collapse of the Qassem regime, the Iraqi government embarked on an Arabization plan which began with the forcible removal of Kurds from the oil-rich regions of Kirkuk, Khanakin, Kifri, Tuz, Pirde, the plains of Arbil, Mahmum, Guer, Dwage, and Karaj.[2] Shortly thereafter, Kurds east of Mosul, Ayn Zaleh, and Sinjar were displaced, and Kurdish land was handed over to Arab settlers. Displaced Kurds were convoyed to the southern deserts and housed in

1. Peter Galbreath and Christopher Van Hollen, Jr., *Chemical Weapons Use in Kurdistan: Iraq's Final Offensive,* staff report to the Committee on Foreign Relations, U.S. Senate, September 21, 1988.

2. For a discussion of this policy, see *The Kurdish Question at the United Nations,* Know the Kurds ser. no. 2, Information Department, Kurdistan Democratic party, June 1974.

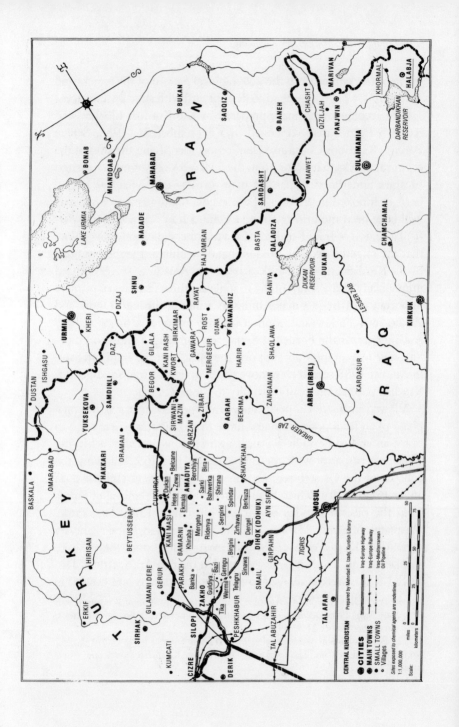

CENTRAL KURDISTAN

Prepared by Mehrdad R. Izady, Kurdish Library

● CITIES
◉ MAIN TOWNS
○ SMALL TOWNS
• Villages

Sites exposed to chemical agents are underlined

1:1,000,000

Iraq-Europe Highway
Iraq-Europe Railway
Iraq-Mediterranean
Oil Pipeline

Scale:
miles 0   25   50
kilometers 0   25   50   75

official detention camps. Some escaped to join the Kurdish forces; others fled to Iran. Escalated in 1974, the first stage reached completion in 1975.

In the same year, the second stage was operationalized with the creation of "security belts" some twenty kilometers in depth running the length of Iraq's borders with Iran, Turkey, and Syria and stretching from Mandali in the south to Shangur in the northwest. Villagers were forcibly removed and detained in government "strategic" villages constructed by the authorities near Arbil, Sulaimania, Chamchamal, Darbandikhan, and Zakho, and on the outskirts of Sinjar and Ayn Sifni. They were left with no belongings other than what they wore and were not permitted to work. Men were given the option of joining the Iraqi army; women and children would remain hostages under government control.

The third stage of the plan commenced in 1985 following a breakdown of negotiations between the government of Saddam Hussein and the leadership of the Patriotic Union of Kurdistan. Within the next two years 781 villages in the Sorani region alone were destroyed. Villagers were driven to remote desert regions near Iraq's borders with Jordan and Saudi Arabia. Arab tribes, primarily Sunnis, were brought in to resettle Kurdish land.

The fourth and final stage has been underway since 1987. In early 1988 four Iraqi army battalions and two armored brigades attacked the Garmian district, destroyed more than 500 villages and 22 towns, confiscated all personal belongings and an estimated 4 million livestock, poisoned water sources, and drove the displaced villagers into the cities. Men were taken as prisoners of war, women and children driven off to destinations unknown. By June 1988, 3,479 of the 5,000 villages extant in 1975 had been destroyed, 825 schools closed, and 2,247 mosques and churches burned to the ground.[3]

The nature and intent of Baghdad's Kurdish policy is evident in an official decision issued on June 14, 1987. Directed to the Com-

3. Author's interview with Jalal Talabani, general secretary of the Patriotic Union of Kurdistan, June 3, 1988.

mittee of Organization leadership of the Zakho Section of National
Defense Battalions, the text reads as follows:

1. It is totally forbidden to allow any foodstuff or person and/or machine to
reach the forbidden villages which are included in the second stage of the
collecting villages. Villagers are allowed to come to the national fold if they
wish, but their relatives are not allowed to contact them without prior no-
tification of the Security apparatus. 2. Existence is totally taboo in the forbidden villages of the first stage. On 21/6/87 begins the second stage of
collecting villages. 3. After harvesting the winter crops which ends before
the 15th of July, cultivation is forbidden for the following summer and
winter seasons. 4. Animal grazing is also forbidden in these areas. 5. It is the
duty of military forces, everyone according to his section, to kill any human
being or animal that exists in these areas which are considered totally forbidden. 6. Those who are included in the deportation orders should be informed and they will be responsible for any misbehavior towards fulfilling
these orders.[4]

Massive human rights abuses against the Kurds over the years
have been documented by Amnesty International. A few examples:
In October 1985 Amnesty reported the abduction of three hundred
children and youths from the city of Sulaimania by the authorities in
an effort to force their relatives in the Kurdish resistance to surrender. The whereabouts of these children was unknown. On February
25, 1987, Amnesty reported that the bodies of seventy-two children
were returned to their families. One month later another twenty-five
bodies were returned, bearing signs of torture, some with their eyes
gouged out. The majority of abductees had been executed. In July
and August of 1983 approximately eight thousand males between
the ages of twelve and eighty belonging to the Barzani tribe were
taken by the authorities from the Qushtapa and Dinaya camps where
they had been detained under government control with their families
since 1978. In large convoys of military trucks they were paraded

4. "Top secret" directive issued by Ali Moashna Kazim, secretary, Committee of
Organizing, National Defense Battalions, Arab Ba'ath Socialist party, no. S/sh/664,
dated June 14, 1987.

through the streets of Baghdad and subsequently driven to a camp near the Jordanian frontier. The whereabouts and fate of these men are still unknown. Amnesty, the U.N. High Commission for Refugees, the International Red Cross, and the International Commission of Jurists were notified of this incident by the Kurds. Amnesty requested that the Iraqi authorities investigate, but no information has been forthcoming. Kurdish sources claim that in 1988 the authorities returned once more to the same camps to reap another harvest of males who had by then reached twelve years of age.

Given this history, it was with dismay that those of us who monitor the Kurdish plight received the news of chemical attacks, which began in earnest in 1987. On April 15, 1987, seven villages in the Sulaimania province were attacked with mustard gas, leaving scores of wounded. On the following day seven villages in the Balisan Valley were bombarded with chemical weapons. The attacks left more than 300 dead and wounded, mainly women and children. In Shaikhwasan alone there were 121 dead including 76 children under eight years of age. Six days of poison gas attacks left behind hundreds of casualties.

On April 21, 1987, the London-based *Independent* reported Kurdish charges that the Iraqi army had deployed chemical weapons against Kurdish civilians. Both the Kurdistan Democratic party and the Patriotic Union of Kurdistan, which constitute the major organized opposition to Iraqi policy, issued urgent appeals to the United Nations and the International Red Cross for observers, gas masks, and humanitarian aid.[5]

Kurdish pleas notwithstanding, international attention to Iraq's deployment of chemical weapons was not forthcoming until almost one year later, following massive media coverage of the March 17, 1988, poison gas attacks on Halabja. The death toll reached an estimated five thousand Kurds, and thousands more were badly in-

5. Patriotic Union of Kurdistan Representation Abroad, "Appeal to the World Public Opinion on the Use of Poison Gas and Chemical Weapons in Iraqi Kurdistan," April 22, 1987.

jured.[6] But international indignation failed to translate into action. Consequently, a little more than five months later the Kurds were again subjected to poison gas attacks. Iraq's chemical offensive began in the final days of August, less than one week after the cease-fire with Iran. On September 1 the *Financial Times* reported that an estimated 100,000 Kurds fled across the border into Turkey, a country that since 1925 has denied any expression of ethnic identity to its indigenous Kurds.

Like the deliberate depopulation of Iraqi Kurdistan, the deployment of chemical weapons was at once denied and justified by the authorities, who claimed that they were destroying guerrilla strongholds, protecting areas threatened by the Iranians, or retaliating against sites captured by Iran with the aid of Iraqi Kurds. "They were supporting the enemy," the *Washington Post* of September 16, 1988, quoted Defense Minister Gen. Adnan Khairallah in an article detailing Baghdad's official denials. It is interesting to note that while Iraqi officials were publicly expressing outrage against Iraqi Kurds for backing the Iranian Pasdaran, the Baghdad government was supporting with aid and free passage the Iranian Kurds who were fighting a guerrilla war against Iran. Landlocked and trapped within the borders of countries that collectively repress their culture and aspirations, the Kurds view themselves as having no choice but to accept aid from whatever quarter offers it.

Baghdad's claim that the August 1988 offensive was intended to crush guerrilla opposition once and for all is of questionable validity. The northern front of Iraq's war against Iran was concentrated in the northeast in the vicinity of the Iraq-Iran border. The August offensive targeted the opposite side of Iraq, bordering Turkey. Backed against an aggressively guarded Turkish border and vulnerable to the control of Baghdad via highway, railway, and easily negotiated terrain, this region was unattractive as a guerrilla base. Moreover, Baghdad was aware that the region's distance from the Iraq-Iran border

6. "New Horrors in a Long-Running Horror Show," *U.S. News and World Report,* April 4, 1988, 59.

discouraged Iranian provocations. In fact, the Kurdish areas slated for destruction in August 1988 were among the most quiescent.

During the course of the war this Kurdish region took on added importance because the Iranian army severed Iraq's access to the Gulf. Deteriorated relations with Syria culminated in the closing of the Iraqi-Syrian oil pipeline. Baghdad was forced to rely solely on the line through Kurdistan to export oil. The facility was in fact expanded. (A parallel oil pipeline was under construction prior to the Gulf War, and a third line is under consideration to carry natural gas through the region.) This Kurdish ancestral land is itself a site of petroleum deposits. Note also that it dominates the northern reaches of Mosul, Iraq's second largest city. During the war, the highway and railway through Iraqi Kurdistan served as Baghdad's route of export and import.

The ultimate irony is that the preponderant supply of oil that has powered the Iraqi state, from the Kirkuk region, rests on traditionally Kurdish land. This is graphically illustrated in maps prepared by the Royal Geographic Society in 1910, maps used by the League of Nations to decide the fate of the Mosul province in the aftermath of World War I. Coveted by the British, Kurdistan's oil deposits were the pivotal factor in the decision of the Allied powers to include the Kurdish vilayet of Mosul within the boundaries of the state of Iraq. According to an Iraqi census of 1922–1924, the population of the Mosul vilayet consisted of 494,007 Kurds and 166,941 Arabs. Nonetheless, the Allied powers determined that the Arab provinces of Basra and Baghdad could not subsist without the economic underpinnings of Mosul's oil wealth. Against their wishes, the Kurds of Mosul were summarily incorporated into the new state, which had been promised to Arabs by the British and the French in return for their active cooperation during the war.

Sir Arnold Wilson, acting civil commissioner in Mesopotamia for His Majesty's government in 1917, summarized the problem in these words: "The idea of Iraq as an independent nation had scarcely taken shape, for the country lacked homogeneity, whether geographical, economic or racial. . . . It was scarcely to be hoped that the vilayets of Basra and Baghdad could maintain their existence as an autonomous state without the revenue it was hoped might eventually be derived from the economic resources of the Mosul vilayet. Yet three-quarters of the inhabitants of the Mosul vilayet were non-Arabs, five-eighths being Kurdish, and one-eighth Christians or Yazidis [non-Islamic Kurds]."[7]

And thus an Arab sheikh from the Hashemite Kingdom was imported from the Arabian Peninsula to govern Iraq under British mandate. His cousin would rule Syria under French tutelage. And the Kurds, who sat on the wealth, would be disfranchised. The cycle of Kurdish uprisings and government repression could have been predicted, but the world outside Iraq paid little attention. Repressing Kurdish aspirations became the task of successive Arab governments, aided and abetted by neighboring Iran, Turkey, and Syria—who had their own Kurdish problems—and by foreign governments with economic and strategic interests in the region.

For more than a decade there have been protests from nongovernmental organizations against continuing violations of Kurdish rights. On January 14, 1977, Roger Baldwin, honorary president of the International League for Human Rights, made this statement in a letter to U.N. Secretary-General Kurt Waldheim: "The enclosed information evidences executions, instances of torture, mass detentions and the deportation of tens of thousands of Kurdish people in an apparent effort to destroy the Kurdish ethnic group." Baldwin's report had been presented to the thirtieth session of the Subcommission on Prevention of Discrimination and Protection of Minorities of the Commission on Human Rights of the United Nations. But that organization continued to dismiss the Kurdish problem in Iraq, and in Iran, Turkey, and Syria, as little more than a nuisance complicating larger issues.

It was fortuitous that the chemical attacks against Halabja were publicized at all. Dubious credit must go to Iran, which seized the

7. Sir Arnold T. Wilson, *Mesopotamia 1917–1920: A Clash of Loyalties; A Personal and Historical Record* (London: Oxford University Press, 1931), x.

occasion to draw attention to Iraq's transgressions. The suffering Kurds were jubilant over the media attention that followed, assuming that sympathy would translate into aid. But international outrage focused instead on Iraq's illegal use of poison gas, and the Kurds descended to a mere footnote to debate over chemical weapons.

The August 1988 Iraqi offensive constitutes the apotheosis of a tyranny unchecked and out of control, thanks to a community of nations that too often operates on the premise that saying something is doing something. Had the United Nations addressed the division and dispossession of the Kurds at an earlier date, there would have been no Halabja. Had the civilized world made a concerted effort to isolate and sanction Iraq after Halabja, August could have been a quiet month.

Nor has there been international concern on purely humanitarian grounds for the plight of more than a half million Iraqi Kurdish refugees waiting without help and without hope in Iran and Turkey—both countries pursuing policies inimical to Kurdish survival, both countries oppressing their indigenous Kurdish populations.

Clearly, the deliberate destruction of a vast segment of the population of Iraqi Kurdistan renders the Baghdad regime in violation of the U.N. Convention on Genocide, as it has violated with impunity international protocols against the use of poison gas. The reluctance of the United Nations to recognize chronic human rights violations against minorities within member states, the neglect of deteriorating situations, and the failure to confront member states engaged in these practices cannot help but send a Machiavellian message to irresponsible regimes contemplating heinous acts in times to come. The tragedy of the Iraqi Kurds can only portend a dismal future for all indigenous peoples who, by virtue of location and resources, obstruct the power paths of nation-states.

René Lemarchand   Chapter 6

BURUNDI: THE POLITICS
OF ETHNIC AMNESIA

AUTHOR'S NOTE: Observing at close range the devastating effects of ethnic
violence in Rwanda and Burundi is what triggered my professional interest
in the study of genocide. Adding to the moral revulsion I felt in the face of
the wanton killing of fellow human beings was the sense of personal tragedy
attendant upon the loss of close friends among Hutu and Tutsi. The mourning of friends transcends ethnic boundaries.

In spite of my continuing involvement in the political fortunes of each
state, as a political scientist I have tried not to let my moral sensibilities get
in the way of a dispassionate analysis of the dynamics of ethnic strife. Shortly
after the publication of my *Rwanda and Burundi* (London: Pall Mall Press,
1970), I was commissioned by the London-based Minority Rights Group
to write a report on the 1972 massacres in Burundi—*Selective Genocide in
Burundi* (London: Minority Rights Group, 1974). Again, following the
1988 killings in Burundi, I was asked to testify before the Subcommittees
on Human Rights and International Organizations of the U.S. House of
Representatives on the roots and implications of the massacre. What follows
is an attempt to put yet another construction on the 1972 and 1988 killings.

Twice in sixteen years Burundi society has been torn to its depths by ethnic conflicts of vast scale. The 1972 bloodbath took the lives of an estimated 100,000, in what must be seen as the closest approximation of an ethnic genocide in postindependence Africa. Informed estimates suggest that in 1988 as many as 20,000 may have been killed by government troops. As in 1972, the overwhelming majority of the victims were of Hutu origins, and so are the thousands of refugees who have fled their homeland.[1] Nowhere in Africa, save perhaps in Ethiopia and the Sudan, have human rights been violated on a more massive scale and with more brutal consistency.

My purpose here is not to pass moral judgment on individuals or institutions; nor is it to chronicle the atrocities committed by each side to the conflict. The aim, in essence, is to expose the extraordinary combination of misperceptions, selective sifting of the evidence, and denial of historical facts that to this day conspires to obfuscate the dynamics or gloss over the reality of ethnic strife in postcolonial Burundi.

That the case of Burundi should have received so little attention in the media is not unrelated to the somewhat arcane image it tends to project—belonging as it were to a residual category of micropolities—such as Equatorial Guinea, Gambia, and Cape Verde—whose minute size and eccentricities are generally seen as sufficient reasons for neglect. But this is at best a partial explanation and at worst an alibi for more fundamental factors and circumstances. To begin with, official accounts of the causes and costs of ethnic conflict are not the most reliable source: as might be expected, the tendency has been to overemphasize the "external subversion" involved in such conflict and to underplay both the saliency of domestic strife and the mag-

---

1. On the 1972 massacre, see René Lemarchand and David Martion, *Selective Genocide in Burundi,* Report no. 20 (London: Minority Rights Group, 1974), and Jeremy Greenland, "Ethnic Discrimination on Rwanda and Burundi," in *Case Studies on Human Rights and Fundamental Freedoms,* vol. 4, ed. Willem A. Veenhoven (The Hague: Martinus Nijhoff, 1976), 95–134. On the 1988 killings, see Filip Reyntjens, "Burundi 1972–1988: Continuité et changement," *Les Cahiers du CEDAF,* no. 5 (November 1989); René Lemarchand, "Burundi: The Killing Fields Revisited," *Issue* 18, no. 1 (Winter 1989): 22–28.

nitude of its human costs. Because the official version is given substantially greater coverage in the media than the views of the victims, the result has generally been to minimize public concern over the depth of the human tragedies involved. By the same token, the public accounts of the victims are by no means free of prejudice and exaggeration. As we shall see, scarcely more illuminating than the image of a society free of ethnic tension is that of one with ancestral enmities built into its "feudal" caste system. Confronted by such contradictory accounts, outside observers often seem at a loss to make sense of the Burundi situation.

Just how far official accounts have shaped Western perceptions of Burundi society is hard to tell; that some observers, however, including academics, have tended to endorse uncritically the myths and misperceptions conveyed by the Bujumbura authorities is undeniable. The self-styled "école historique burundo-française," a small group of French historians with close ties to the government and the University of Burundi, is notable for how it reproduces the official biases. Their denial that ethnicity is a major source of conflict in Burundi belies their claim to scientific objectivity. Nothing is more detrimental to the intellectual responsibility of scholars than the enticement of praise-singing as a means of securing the favors and friendship of officialdom, along with guarantees of continued access to the field.[2]

More complex is the case of development experts, most of whom have remained prudently silent about the Burundi tragedies. Though possibly reflecting pragmatic considerations similar to those noted above, their discretion is also traceable to the notion, especially prevalent among development economists, that there is a necessary trade-off between equity and economic growth. Inasmuch as the social

2. See, e.g., Jean-Pierre Chrétien and Gabriel Le Jeune, "Developpement rural et democratie paysanne, un dilemme? L'exemple du Burundi," *Politique Africaine*, no. 11 (September 1983): 45–76. For a critical commentary of the "école historique burundo-francaise," see René Lemarchand, "L'école historique burundo-française: Une école pas comme les autres," *Canadian Journal of African Studies* (forthcoming); Filip Reyntjens, "Du bon usage de la science: L'école historique burundo-francaise," *Politique Africaine,* no. 37 (March 1990): 107–112.

structure of Burundi exemplifies a highly institutionalized form of ethnic inequality (of which more in a moment), the more objection-able features of this situation are generally seen as the price that must be paid for improving levels of economic growth and efficiency. Be-hind this reasoning lies a kind of self-fulfilling prophecy: as privi-leged recipients of wealth and education, members of the ruling mi-nority (Tutsi) are by force of circumstances the chief promoters of economic development. Small wonder if, as one World Bank official tersely observed, "the level of education among the Tutsi is extraor-dinary; it makes for a damned good administration."[3] So good in-deed that Burundi ranked in 1988 as one of the highest per capita recipients of International Development Agency (IDA) loans in the world. And it is one of the few states of Africa to have put into effect the economic reforms advocated by the bank. But if, in the light of these achievements, some do not hesitate to associate Tutsi suprem-acy with economic performance, it is perhaps even more to the point to note that ethnic supremacy lies at the very heart of the 1972 and 1988 crises.

Before moving on to a discussion of the genesis of conflict, several important caveats are in order. To begin with, relatively little is said herin of the post-1988 efforts of the Buyoya government to initiate reforms designed to mitigate intergroup tensions—not because these efforts are unimportant, but mainly for reasons of space.[4] Much of what follows, therefore, focuses on the 1972–1988 period. More-over, though my main concern is with the tendency of the ruling group (and its foreign "clients") to deny or at least minimize the salience of ethnic conflict, it is worth reiterating that "the view from below" is by no means free of biases of the opposite kind. Myth-

3. Quoted in Blaine Harden, "Moneylenders Horrified by the Burundi Kill-ings," *Washington Post,* September 4, 1988.

4. For further details, see René Lemarchand, "The Burundi National Commis-sion on National Unity: A Critical Commentary," *Journal of Modern African Studies* 27, no. 4 (1989): 685–690. The report of the commission is available in English in a mimeographed document issued by the Burundi embassy in Washington, *Presenta-tion of the Report of the National Commission to Study the Question of National Unity* (Bujumbura: May 19, 1989), 28.

making is alive and well on both sides of the ethnic divide. Finally, the risks of reductionism are all too plain when one seeks to identify the members of a given ethnic community with a specific set of perceptions or misperceptions. Efforts at generalization on that score are made in full recognition that they can be challenged on the familiar grounds that there are exceptions to every rule—and indeed in the hope that the exceptions may some day become the rule.

THE GENESIS OF CONFLICT: MYTHS AND REALITIES

One of the least controversial propositions about Burundi society (though based on census figures dating back to the colonial period) is that it consists of a majority of Hutu (about 85 percent), with the Tutsi accounting for 14 percent and the pygmoid Twa for 1 percent of a total population of approximately 5 million. But these are very rough estimates. Left out of the accounting are an undetermined number of individuals of mixed and princely (*ganwa*) origins, as well as a substantial sprinkling of Swahili-speaking and other immigrant communities. Where disagreements persist is on the characterization of Hutu and Tutsi as social categories and the nature of their relationship with each other. Out of these disagreements—critically related to the time span in which conflict developed—have emerged two radically different, and equally misleading, interpretations of the roots of ethnic crises.

In much of the official literature published by Hutu opposition movements in exile, most notably the *Parti pour l'emancipation du peuple Hutu (Palipehutu)*, the 1972 and 1988 killings are viewed as historically linked to the centuries-old domination of the Tutsi minority, alternatively described as a "tribe" or a "caste." From this perspective the killings are only the most recent and brutal manifestation of Tutsi efforts to perpetuate their "tribal" hegemony in the face of Hutu demands for full participation in the political life of the country. This construction, as Liisa Malkki convincingly demonstrates, is part and parcel of a "mythico-history" that has developed principally among Hutu refugee communities in the wake of the

1972 slaughter. What is involved here is "not only a description of the past, nor even merely an evaluation of the past, but a subversive recasting and reinterpreting of it in fundamentally moral terms."[5]

Inasmuch as one can speak of an official Tutsi position, it rests on a totally different view of history, one that emphasizes the organic unity of Hutu and Tutsi: because of their shared linguistic and socio-cultural affinities, neither group fits the defining characteristics of a "tribe." Only through the divide-and-rule policies of the Belgian colonizer could the inner cohesion of Burundi society be seriously threatened. Citing the case of neighboring Rwanda, where Belgian intervention was a major contributory factor in the overthrow of the Tutsi monarchy and its replacement by a Hutu-dominated republic, the standard argument advanced by Tutsi officials is that the 1972 and 1988 crises were the consequence of the provocations and incitements of a tiny group of Hutu malcontents seeking to emulate the Rwanda model. In this alternative version of "mythico-history" it is not only the cultural boundaries between Hutu and Tutsi that are deliberately glossed over but the drastic reordering of ethnic identities brought about by the 1972 killings.

Although neither explanation is entirely satisfactory, both are partially correct. Although the case for caste is simply inarguable as a characteristic feature of traditional society, the term *tribe* is hardly more serviceable to describe communities that share the same language, the same clan structure, and at one time the same commitment to monarchical symbols, not to mention their close physical intermingling in most rural settings. The case for an age-old domination of the Hutu masses by the Tutsi minority is hardly more convincing.[6] Besides misleadingly suggesting an immutable commit-

5. Liisa Helena Malkki, "Purity and Exile: Transformations in Historical National Consciousness among Hutu Refugees in Tanzania" (Ph.D. diss., Harvard University, 1989; Ann Arbor: University Microfilms, 1989), 125; forthcoming publication by University of Chicago Press, 1992.

6. The key power holders in precolonial and colonial Burundi were known as *ganwa,* or princes, and were seen by themselves as well as by Hutu and Tutsi as culturally and socially distinct from either group. For further information, see René Lemarchand, *Rwanda and Burundi* (London: Pall Mall Press, 1971).

ment to primordial sentiments, the term *tribe* normally refers to a territorially bounded and culturally discrete entity. In this sense, to speak of Hutu and Tutsi as "tribes" is of course arrant nonsense. On the other hand, there can be little doubt that in the years following independence, particularly from 1972 to 1988, Burundi society transformed itself into a rigidly stratified social order in which status, power, and authority tended to gravitate to Tutsi hands. At this point ethnic self-awareness, once politically mobilized, gained unprecedented weight in the structuring of state authority.

The rise of Tutsi hegemony might conceivably be seen as paving the way for the emergence of a "ruling caste," but it is the novelty of the phenomenon that needs to be stressed rather than its historical depth. Thus, rather than treat mobilized ethnicity as a historical datum, a more useful perspective is to recognize the critical role played by aspiring politicians, both Hutu and Tutsi, in mobilizing ethnic identities. That ethnic polarization did receive a major impetus from the projection of the Rwanda model into the domestic arena of Burundi is undeniable. Despite the greater complexity of its ethnic map and the absence of rigid divisions of the kind that characterized pre-revolutionary Rwanda, the Burundi social system could not be but profoundly affected by the political message of the Hutu revolution in neighboring Rwanda. While providing the nascent Hutu elites of Burundi with the "model polity" that some tried to emulate, it also gave the Tutsi elites ample justification for their incipient fears of Hutu domination.

Although seldom recognized by Tutsi commentators, several critical developments occurred in 1965 whose cumulative effects decisively accelerated the trend toward ethnic polarization.[7] The assassination of Pierre Ngendadumwe, the first Hutu prime minister since independence (1962), in January 1965 at the hands of a Tutsi refugee from Rwanda was the initial catalyst behind the crystallization of a Hutu political consciousness. The second major event took place shortly after the legislative elections of May 1965, which brought a

7. For a fuller treatment, see ibid.

two-thirds Hutu majority into the National Assembly: the decision of King *(mwami)* Mwambutsa to disregard their victory at the polls by appointing one of his closest courtiers, Leopold Bihumugani, to the post of prime minister effectively robbed the Hutu of their electoral victory while converting the parliament into a rubber stamp. On October 18, 1965, Hutu anger broke out in an abortive coup directed against the king's palace, followed by sporadic attacks against Tutsi elements in the interior.

In reprisal Tutsi units of the army and gendarmerie arrested and shot eighty-six leading Hutu politicians and officers. With the threat of a Hutu takeover temporarily removed, the Tutsi-dominated army then turned against the monarchy. On November 28, while attending the first anniversary celebrations of Mobutu's military takeover in Kinshasa, Mwambutsa's successor on the throne, Charles Ndizeye, learned from a radio broadcast that the army had deposed him and proclaimed Burundi a republic. From then on all powers were concentrated in a Tutsi-dominated National Revolutionary Council, headed by Captain (now President) Michel Micombero. After the discovery of an alleged Hutu plot in 1969, some thirty Hutu personalities, civilian and military, were immediately executed, thus making the trend toward Tutsi supremacy all the more evident. As one observer commented, "Practically no Hutu received scholarships to study abroad after 1968, while a bizarre 'girth by height' requirement was introduced as a patent pretext for excluding unwanted Hutu recruits from the army."[8]

This is not the place for a detailed account of the complex intra-Tutsi squabbles and maneuverings that preceded the 1972 massacre and may have prompted the few remaining Hutu leaders to exploit the situation to their advantage.[9] Suffice it to note that the crisis was triggered by a series of indiscriminate attacks by Hutu insurgents against Tutsi civilians in the capital city of Bujumbura as well as in many of the provinces. In its initial stages the rebellion is said to have cost at least 2,000 Tutsi lives, with Bururi claiming the heaviest

8. Greenland, "Ethnic Discrimination," 119.
9. See Lemarchand and Martin, *Selective Genocide in Burundi*.

losses. The scale of the repression proved even more devastating. Indeed, what followed was not so much repression as a systematic slaughter of all educated and semieducated Hutu elements. In Bujumbura, Gitega, and Ngozi all "cadres" of Hutu origins, including not only local civil servants but schoolchildren, chauffeurs, clerks, and skilled workers, were rounded up, taken to jail, and either shot or beaten to death with rifle butts. In Bujumbura alone an estimated 4,000 Hutu were loaded up in trucks and taken to their graves. Precise estimates of the number of Hutu killed are nowhere to be found. The figure most frequently quoted—100,000—probably errs on the conservative side, whereas the number advanced by members of the Palipehutu—400,000—appears to be wildly exaggerated. What is beyond dispute is that the drastic surgery performed by the army effectively removed the menace of what many Tutsi now referred to as *"le peril Hutu,"* at least in the short run. Not until 1988 would the peril again loom on the horizon, and with similarly tragic consequences.

PATTERNS OF VIOLENCE: 1972 AND 1988

It may be useful at this point to take a retrospective look at the events of 1972 and 1988, if only to identify the similarities and differences between them. Although there is no gainsaying the fact of Tutsi oppression underlying these events, the context in which they occurred, the precipitating factors behind them, and the resulting scale of violence suggest significant variations.

The critical difference between the 1972 and 1988 killings is that they occurred in radically different political contexts. Although violence was in each case preceded by major discord among the ruling elites, there was no equivalent in 1972 for the move toward "liberalization" initiated by President Pierre Buyoya after seizing power from Jean-Baptiste Bagaza in September 1987. As is now becoming increasingly clear, Buyoya's call for a more liberal stance on the issue of Hutu-Tutsi relations had little impact on local Tutsi functionaries, most of whom stuck to a rigidly discriminatory posture. Hutu expectations were raised to an unprecedented level, causing some of them to appeal to Bujumbura, but their hopes remained largely unfulfilled and their demands unmet.

The challenge faced by the Buyoya regime in 1988 was entirely different from that faced by Micombero in 1972, when coordinated attacks against Tutsi elements were launched in several localities at the instigation of Hutu leaders and for the specific purpose of capturing power. In 1988 the initial attacks against Tutsi civilians were more in the nature of a spontaneous outburst of rage, triggered by the provocations of a local Tutsi personality and fueled by rumors of an impending massacre of Hutu peasants.

The precipitating event took place in the commune of Ntega on August 14, when, according to one observer, a rich coffee merchant, a Tutsi named Reverien Harushinguro, "said to have been involved with the killings in 1972, refused to pay some Hutu peasants money he owed them. He taunted them, then shot and killed five."[10] Revenge quickly ensued. After killing the trader and his family, bands of Hutu armed with clubs, spears, machetes, and bows and arrows set fire to Tutsi homes and killed the occupants.

Meanwhile, a few miles away, in the commune of Marangara, Hutu-Tutsi tensions had already reached their peak. At issue here was the presence in this commune of four Tutsi civil servants, including the mayor, a judge, and a medical assistant, whose anti-Hutu sentiments were well known. On June 28 the mayor made an inflammatory speech that convinced many Hutu that a plan was afoot to wipe them out. "You are preparing your knives," the mayor is reported to have said, "but ours are sharper and cut more than yours." Hutu appeals to Bujumbura to have the mayor dismissed proved unavailing. And when three army vehicles appeared on the scene, on August 5, following what some described as "a mild uprising," panic broke out. "We knew what they were going to do," said one refugee interviewed in Rwanda. "Everyone was saying: 1972! 1972!"[11]

10. Catherine Watson, "After the Massacre," *Africa Report,* January-February 1989, 54.

11. Ibid.

In the climate of intense fear that spread through Marangara and the neighboring communes, almost any incident could trigger a violent reaction. The incident came with the provocations of Reverien Harushinguro, the Tutsi merchant from Ntega. Thus, though originating in different arenas and out of separate issues, ethnic hatreds suddenly surged in the form of a blind fury directed against every Tutsi in sight. As many as five hundred may have been killed in Ntega and its vicinity. The restoring of "peace and order" by the army proved even more horrendous. Assisted by helicopters and armored vehicles, Buyoya's troops unleashed their retribution with appalling brutality. According to Amnesty International, "The scale of resistance offered to the soldiers is not known, but the inclusion of large numbers of women and children among their victims suggests that troops were engaged not just in quelling armed resistance or indeed in searching for those who had participated in killings of Tutsi, but rather in reprisals aimed at the Hutu civilian population as a whole and carried out to punish and eliminate them rather than just to restore public order." [12] In short, the 1972 repression came about in response to an organized conspiracy against the state; the 1988 repression followed in the wake of a disorganized display of rural violence directed against local officials.

In the popular consciousness of the Hutu masses, forebodings of an impending bloodbath, comparable to what had happened in 1972, played a key role in the *grande peur* phenomenon that led to the indiscriminate killing of Tutsis in the Ntega commune in August 1988. An isolated act of violence by a single individual of Tutsi origins thus was widely perceived as the premonitory sign of a reenactment of the 1972 killings. Panic spread through the Hutu community. Partly out of an uncontrolled fear of what might happen next, partly out of a sense of outrage, some Hutu extremists unleashed their fury against innocent Tutsi, killing scores of them and thus bringing down a devastating retribution.

Whereas in 1972 almost every region and locality, including the

12. Amnesty International, *Burundi: Killings of Children by Government Troops*, AFR. 16/04, 1988, 3.

capital, was targeted for the physical liquidation of all educated Hutu elements down to the primary school level, in 1988 repressive violence was both more indiscriminate and more localized. Again to quote from the Amnesty International report, "More and more evidence has become available that members of Burundi's armed forces were responsible for massive numbers of executions of unarmed civilians, and that many of the victims were young children, some of them babies, who had played no part in any of the preceding violence. They were selected for execution simply because they and their parents were Hutu and lived in an area in which members of the Hutu community had attacked and killed Tutsi."[13]

THE POLITICS OF ETHNIC AMNESIA

For all the differences notes above, official responses to the 1972 and 1988 crises have been remarkably consistent (at least until October 1988): even when confronted with the most dramatic evidence of ethnic conflict, officials repeatedly denied the existence of separate ethnic identities.

Not until October 1988, and after considerable pressure from both the U.S. Congress and the State Department, did President Buyoya finally concede the existence of an ethnic problem: on October 6 a consultative commission of twenty-four members, including an equal number of Tutsi and Hutu, was appointed to investigate the circumstances of the massacre and make appropriate recommendations; shortly thereafter, on October 12, Buyoya agreed to a major reshuffling of his cabinet, increasing the number of Hutu ministers from six to twelve, with the prime ministership in the hands of a Hutu (Adrien Sibomana).

Until then, however, ethnic differences simply did not exist. In August 1988, when asked by a journalist what proportion of Hutu and Tutsi had been killed, Buyoya laconically brushed aside the question: "We are all Burundi," he replied. The assumption, in short, has

13. Ibid., 1.

been that by eliminating all public references to ethnic identities, ethnic discrimination will no longer matter either as a policy issue or as a source of intergroup conflict. Proceeding from the axiom that ethnic labels and stereotypes belong to the dustbin of colonial historiography, the official view until recently was that ethnic references are at best a figment of the colonial imagination, at worst part of a neocolonial stratagem designed to play one group of citizens off against another. That ethnic identities might have taken on a new reality in the years that followed independence, through processes of political mobilization and class formation, was never seriously considered.

But if ethnic conflict, like ethnic discrimination, is at best an epiphenomenon, what is the explanation for the 1972 and 1988 killings? The answer is found in a document titled "A Critical Reflection on the Recent Events of Ntega and Marangara," written by a group of predominantly Tutsi professors at the University of Bujumbura: "tribal ideology." Rejecting as "spurious explanations" the twofold argument of Tutsi oppression and the absence of democracy, "tribal ideology" is said to include "two major components: the imposition of the ethnic factor as an element of political legitimacy, and a plot [projet] aimed at the physical elimination of all Tutsi."[14] Both aspects were present in the abortive 1965 coup, described as a *coup d'état tribal,* and again in the 1969 plot, which paved the way for the "sad events of 1972." Insofar as "it advocates the physical elimination of the Tutsi, this tribal ideology carries a tragic corollary: genocide."[15] Thus if the term *genocide* has any meaningful application to the Burundi situation, it is to be found not in the scale of Tutsi repression but in the murderously conspiratorial nature of the "tribal ideology" propagated by "Hutu ideologues." Interestingly, though starting from a diametrically opposed postulate (the presence of ancestral tribal hatreds based on Tutsi oppression), much the same kind

14. Liboire Kagabo et al., "A propos des recents événements de Ntega et Marangara: Une reflexion critique" (Bujumbura, 1988), mimeo. In the same interpretive mold, see "Burundi: Un seul peuple," *Echo de l'Union des Etudiants Stagiaires Burundais à Québec,* no. 1 (October 1988).

15. Kagabo, "A propos des recents événements," 15.

of conspiracy theory is endorsed by many Hutu: the so-called Sim-bananiye plan (after Artemon Simbananiye, a noted Tutsi hardliner and former cabinet minister who played a key role in organizing the 1972 massacres) has been repeatedly invoked as "proof" of a Tutsi-sponsored plot to eliminate physically half of the Hutu popula-tion![16]

The emphasis placed by the authors on the role of Hutu ideo-logues and extremists in plotting the physical elimination of the Tutsi rules out the notion of ethnic conflict. The latter suggests a widely shared sense of "us against them" as well as a high degree of cultural or political self-awareness. Neither condition really fits the Burundi situation. Since "there is no trace of oppression of the majority by the minority"[17] but only a distribution of responsibilities according to merit, there is no basis for ethnic conflict. External subversion, relayed by local Hutu extremists, is thus the only plausible ex-planation for the "recurrent maladies" that have affected Burundi society.

Surprisingly, official denials of ethnicity as a source of conflict have found a highly receptive echo in the works of at least some social scientists. Here the case of the leading exponent of the so-called école historique burundo-française, Professor Jean-Pierre Chrétien, deserves special consideration as the most egregious ex-ample of academic sycophancy in French historiography. After twenty years of sustained research into the history and politics of the coun-try, he has probably a better grasp of the political realities of contem-porary Burundi than any other scholar. Yet nowhere in his pre-1988 writings is there the slightest intimation of the ethnic crisis facing the country, much less of an awareness of possible solutions; no-where is there anything like a recognition of the potential for ethnic violence generated by the discriminatory policies followed by every government since 1972. For Chrétien, as for the majority of Burundi

16. For a further elaboration on the Simbabaniye plan and some gruesome illus-trations of what the author refers to as "the mythico-history of atrocity," see Malkki, "Purity and Exile," 183 ff.

17. Kagabo, "A propos des recents événements," 7.

officials, including his former student, a one-time executive secretary of the ruling party, Etienne Mworoha, the Hutu-Tutsi question is a false problem, created out of whole cloth by European missionaries.[18]

Over the past decade Chrétien has written extensively on Burundi, but not without generating intense controversy over what one critic, Roger Botte, described as an "enterprise of disinformation."[19] Botte's strictures were inspired by a joint article published in 1983 by Chrétien and Gabriel Le Jeune purporting to show that the communal congresses held in 1981 under the auspices of the ruling party, the Union pour le Progrès National (Uprona), captured the essence of a peasant democracy aimed at rural development.[20] The article, like the proceedings of the congresses on which it is based, remains utterly silent on the subject of Hutu-Tutsi relations. As the title of Botte's rejoinder cruelly suggests ("When the essential remains unsaid"), the authors' discussion is fatally flawed by their refusal to acknowledge the centrality of ethnic issues. That these are indeed of critical importance to an understanding of local issues was made dramatically clear by the events of August 1988 in Ntega and Marangara.

The issue at stake here is not just one of shoddy scholarship. What is at stake is the responsibility of scholars in contributing to our understanding of crisis situations involving the fate and life chances of thousands of human beings. It brings into focus the basic choices that need to be made between the exigencies of scholarly objectivity and fair-mindedness, on the one hand, and the temptations of apologetics, on the other.

The critical question raised by the 1972 and 1988 tragedies— what can be done to promote democratic change in the midst of institutionalized ethnic inequality—has been consistently evaded not

18. See Lemarchand, "L'école historique burundo-française."

19. Roger Botte, "Quand l'essentiel n'est pas ce que l'on dit, mais ce que l'on tait," *Politique Africaine,* no. 12 (December 1983): 99–104.

20. Chrétien and Le Jeune, "Developpement rural et democratie paysanne, un dilemme?" 45–76.

just by academics but by development experts, with the result that development aid has tended to perpetuate and in a sense legitimize existing power relationships.

The reasons for this are complex and go far beyond the obvious conclusion that Tutsi elements usually end up being the privileged recipients of aid benefits. A more relevant consideration, as noted earlier, has to do with the trade-off between efficiency and inequality that seems to govern the thinking of many development economists as well as their relationships with the host government. On this premise human rights issues are often sacrificed on the altar of economic performance. Burundi is no exception. "I am a bit shocked by the whole thing," said a World Bank official in the wake of the 1988 killings, "because we are supporting this system."[21] Possibly mitigating his sense of shock, however, was the realization that, as one journalist noted, "the well-organized, well-managed and relatively uncorrupt Tutsi government has been extraordinarily receptive to the bank's free-market dogma. . . . Burundi has devalued its currency, eliminated most important restrictions, raised prices paid to farmers and stripped the economy of regulations that inhibit trade."[22] Compliance paid off handsomely. No sooner had Buyoya seized power than the bank granted his government a three-year $90 million structural-adjustment loan.

To put the matter in the mildest terms, the concept of project development as advocacy enjoys very low priority among international donors. Neglect of the socioethnic parameters within which aid projects are formulated and implemented has been a recurrent characteristic of most development efforts, with the consequence that there has been remarkably little concern over monitoring the social impact of such efforts.

Dismal as it may sound, the conclusion that suggests itself is that few people care, and fewer still know enough about the country to challenge public indifference about its destiny. Even among those who are most knowledgeable about the history and politics of the

21. Blaine Harden, "Moneylenders."
22. Ibid.

country something approximating a conspiracy of silence surrounds the subject of Hutu-Tutsi relations.

The most significant departure from the generalized public indifference about Burundi came in September 1988, in the course of a congressional hearing that led to the passage of a nonbinding resolution by the House of Representatives. In it the House

urged the government of Burundi to maintain and greatly increase its recent efforts at national reconciliation . . . condemned the recent violence reportedly carried out by the armed forces . . . and urged the President and Secretary of State to conduct a comprehensive reassessment of the United States' bilateral relationship with the Government of Burundi with a view towards the immediate suspension of U.S. assistance (other than humanitarian aid) unless within six months after the date of this resolution (a) an impartial enquiry . . . has been initiated to determine the causes of the outbreaks of violence; (b) the Government of Burundi has taken steps to investigate and prosecute those military and administrative officials and private individuals responsible for the recent atrocities. . . ; (c) the Government of Burundi has made substantial progress in promoting the safe return to their homes of Burundi's refugee population. . . ; (d) the Government of Burundi continues to grant foreign journalists and international humanitarian relief organizations free access to the areas affected by recent violence.[23]

The most significant aspect of the present situation is not that some of these recommendations have yet to be put into effect but the extent to which they have been complied with. Whether, as a result of these reforms, significant changes will take place in the distribution of rank and privilege is hard to tell. Although there can be little question about the trend toward ethnic depolarization, memories of the 1972 and 1988 killings will persist for generations, and so will the mutual fears and hatreds they have instilled in the minds of the Burundi. For years to come the past will indeed continue to haunt Burundi's political future, shaping its ethnic destinies in ways that are as yet impossible to predict.

23. For the full text of the resolution, see Lemarchand, "Burundi: The Killing Fields Revisited," 28.

Walter K. Ezell   *Chapter 7*

NEWSPAPER RESPONSES TO REPORTS OF ATROCITIES: BURUNDI, MOZAMBIQUE, IRAQ

AUTHOR'S NOTE: I became interested in genocide after observing the world's weak response to the massacre of over a million people in East Pakistan in 1971. Other cases that stirred me were those of Uganda and Cambodia. After observing in 1984 that there was still very little comparative study of genocide, I left my job as a magazine editor to devote several years to research. Now I work as a copy editor and wire editor, monitoring the wire services and selecting national and international stories for publication in the *Greenville* (S.C.) *Piedmont*. I have published a few scholarly articles and have compiled a catalog of about forty cases and a broad-ranging genocide bibliography listing fifteen hundred items.

A separate bibliography I prepared for this article is too long for publication here. For a copy, please send a self-addressed envelope with two ounces' worth of postage to Walter K. Ezell, 118 Spring Valley Road, Greenville, SC 29615.

For human rights advocates and other concerned people, newspaper reports may be the first indication that a war, famine, or ethnic conflict is genocidal. This chapter traces and analyzes newspaper coverage of three 1988 cases: the conflict between Hutus and Tutsis in Burundi; Mozambique rebel atrocities against civilians, as described in a U.S. State Department paper; and Iraq's gassing of Kurds.

In preparing this chapter I searched the indexes of five major American newspapers covering a fifteen-month period to assemble a bibliography of articles on these three cases. The pattern of the newspapers' coverage, how it intensifies during and falls off after a major development, is illustrated in the figures in this chapter. On the basis of an examination of all the headlines and some of the articles related to those cases, this chapter asks how the newspapers characterized each event—as civil war, famine, massacre, atrocity, ethnic conflict, or genocide—and considers how these characterizations change in response to new information.

It may be years—if ever—before a scholarly consensus is reached on whether certain atrocities are properly called genocide, but the urgency of the need for rescue usually leaves no time for debate over terminology. Like firefighters trained to treat every alarm as a genuine emergency, scholars and advocates need to respond to warning signs as if the worst were possible. For purposes of this essay, I have selected several cases that have not been proven or generally accepted to be genocide. But they involve conflict and the deaths of many group members; and there are allegations of genocide and evidence that warrant investigation.

Newspaper accounts of genocide can alert activists and authorities in a position to do something about the atrocities. Because scholars, seeking an explanation for the inadequate response of activists and authorities, sometimes examine newspapers to see how much was or could have been known at the time, the question arises, how effectively are newspapers reporting cases that are of interest to genocide investigators? We can break down that question into several more specific ones pertaining to the three cases discussed here:

1. What was the pattern of coverage? The important considera-tion here is time: for each day's delay in reporting atrocities and acting on those reports, more lives may be lost. As the figures accom-panying this chapter demonstrate, events involving great human suf-fering and loss of life tend to be covered in spurts. The massacres in Burundi amounted to a three-week succession of blips on the radar screen of current events; the study found only a few follow-up arti-cles about ethnic conflict in Burundi during the fifteen-month pe-riod. The story of Kurds was covered more intensively and exten-sively, but only in September 1988. After that, the coverage evolved into a new story: international efforts to eliminate biological and chemical weapons. Coverage of the civil war in Mozambique came in a succession of one- to five-week spurts, one of them following the release of a State Department report, another when Pope John Paul II visited the region.

2. What prompted the initial coverage and each successive spurt of coverage? In other words, what focuses the attention of American newspaper editors and their readers on atrocities in remote regions? Knowing what causes a story to break can help human rights advo-cates ensure that cases break as early as possible and that none is overlooked.

3. What policy issues did these reports raise? For example, gov-ernments may debate whether to impose sanctions, send aid to the victims, or intervene in some other way.

4. How were the major actors and their roles characterized in these cases? Each produced its own set of ambiguities, some delib-erately fostered by the perpetrators of the atrocities. Until outsiders have a clear picture of what has happened, they may waver about what action to take.

5. To what extent did the initial spurt of coverage resolve the ambiguities?

During a relatively brief period of time, an atrocity is publicized, reporters and others try to learn what has happened, and outsiders decide on the basis of that information whether to act and what actions to take. Thus we have a three-part process—discovery, investigation, and action. Understanding the brevity of this process leads to this study's major recommendation—that trained investigative teams be prepared to respond as soon as an atrocity is reported, resolving ambiguity early, during the first spurt of news coverage, and thus allowing onlookers to decide quickly whether and how to act on the basis of reliable information. This rapid deployment of fact finders is an essential element of any genocide early-warning system.

Four of the five daily newspapers whose coverage I analyzed— the *Christian Science Monitor, Los Angeles Times, New York Times,* and *Washington Post*—offer regular international coverage and can be expected to cover wars, ethnic conflicts, and atrocities. All four papers offer syndication of their news articles, and many U.S. newspapers subscribe to some of those syndication services. The fifth newspaper surveyed, the *Wall Street Journal,* mentions such cases occasionally on its news pages and sometimes quite eloquently on its editorial pages. These are the five newspapers included in the National Newspaper Index (NNI), accessible in libraries through the Infotrac computerized data base and via computer modem through Dialog Information Services and the Knowledge Index Service. The NNI includes the usual bibliographic information plus the length (in column inches) of each article. Column widths and type sizes vary from paper to paper and even within a newspaper, of course, so column measurement is not exact, but its ready availability makes it a useful analytical tool. The numbers graphically show the pattern of coverage in each case. The search of the NNI was supplemented by a search of separate indexes for each newspaper, and some articles, mostly wire stories and briefs, were added to the bibliography. For some of these added articles, I used the word counts furnished in the indexes to determine approximate length in column inches.

ETHNIC MASSACRES IN BURUNDI

Long-standing ethnic tensions in Burundi flared into massacres August 14, 1988. The killings went unnoticed in the United States—and presumably most of the world—for nearly a week (see fig. 7.1). On August 20 the *New York Times* published an Associated Press report datelined Nairobi, Kenya, based on reports by "diplomats and opposition leaders," and the *Los Angeles Times* published a Reuter report. In the AP article diplomats quoted refugees from both tribes as saying that "thousands" had been killed. The article also recounted an August 18 interview with Burundi's ambassador to Belgium. The Reuter piece cited an August 18 statement by the official Burundi news agency, Agence Burundaise de Presse, and an apparently subsequent statement by an exile group in Brussels known as the Hutu People's Liberation Army. Thus in both stories the earliest source for which a date is cited is the Burundi government. It is

Figure 7.1. Ethnic massacres in Burundi: A pattern of coverage by four major newspapers, August 20–October 21, 1988

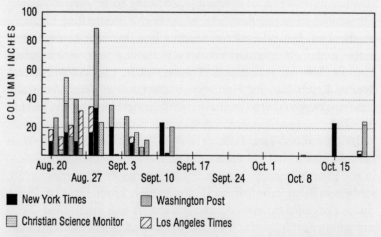

New York Times ■
Christian Science Monitor
Washington Post
Los Angeles Times

Note: Each bar represents a day. After three weeks of coverage, Burundi returned to obscurity. On October 19, Burundi's president named a new prime minister.

not clear what prompted the government statements four days after the massacres began. It is possible, but by no means clear from these articles, that it was the exodus of refugees that brought the story to the world's attention. In any case, refugees and those who talked with them provided the major alternative to government accounts of the massacres.

The *Washington Post* weighed in a day after the *New York Times* with a report, also datelined Nairobi, that an estimated six hundred to eight hundred people had been killed, with the possibility that more bodies would be found—a casualty estimate reflecting the sketchiness of initial reports. The representative of the U.N. High Commission for Refugees in neighboring Rwanda said that refugees had been arriving at the rate of five thousand a day.

On August 23 the story moved onto the front pages of the *New York Times* and the *Washington Post*. The *Post* story, which gained great immediacy from its interviews with refugees, led with a report that "Burundi's armed forces, using 20th century weapons to continue an ancient feud, have deployed helicopters to gun down peasants fleeing from tribal massacres, according to refugee accounts." The article, from the Reuter news agency, was datelined Kigali, in neighboring Rwanda, where refugees had fled. The second paragraph contained information from a Burundi government briefing. The story also cited refugees as claiming that Burundian soldiers went door to door bayoneting Hutu men, women, and children, and quoted one refugee who claimed to have been bayoneted by soldiers and left for dead.

By November, Jane Perlez, the *New York Times* bureau chief in Nairobi, had sorted out events and gave details in an extended piece in the paper's Sunday magazine of November 6. In August 1988, soldiers of the reformist Burundi government headed by Maj. Pierre Buyoya engaged in unannounced maneuvers that interrupted coffee smuggling into Rwanda. A Tutsi provincial administrator reportedly told disgruntled Hutu, "We know you're sharpening your knives, but our knives are already sharp, and they cut more than yours." Word of the remark spread, and Hutu attacked Tutsi with machetes, spears, and stones. The army is dominated by Tutsis and when soldiers came in to restore order they retaliated with wholesale massacres.[1]

An analysis of headlines on Burundi stories showed that eight characterized the killings as "tribal warfare," "tribal violence," "tribal hatreds," and so on, without indicating a perpetrator. Another eight gave an even more neutral characterization—for example, "massacres" or "thousands killed"—again without indicating a perpetrator. One headline spoke ambiguously of "Hutu massacres," and another mentioned "Tutsi domination." Six headlines indicated, with varying degrees of intensity, army participation in the killings: "Army Puts Down Strife, Said to Begin with a Hutu Attack on Tutsi"; "Helicopters Are New Weapon in Ancient Feud"; "Burundi Army Reportedly Took Part in Massacre"; "Burundi Leader Tells of Army Reprisals"; "Burundi Leader Concedes Troops Killed Civilians"; and "Army May Have Added to Revenge in Burundi." Four headlines referred to the government's version of what started the outbreak—"Hutu Attack on Tutsi"; "Exiled Dissidents"; "Machete Attack"; "Invading Rebels"—and one reported, "Burundi Rejects Outside Investigation of Massacres." Five had Burundi disclosing bad news (including the above-quoted presidential admissions of army killings), showing an awareness that a degree of openness would help the government's credibility.

In early reporting, speculation on the causes was shaded by the Burundi government version that exiled Hutus had returned and incited the Hutu population to massacre Tutsis. The government version differed from Perlez's wrap-up piece in at least two important respects: (1) the question of whether it was a Tutsi administrator or returning Hutu exiles who had incited the initial Hutu attacks on Tutsis, and (2) whether soldiers in the Tutsi-dominated army showed restraint or retaliated with wholesale massacres. Burundi government spokesmen were more defensive and less open than the

1. Jane Perlez, "The Bloody Hills of Burundi: Long-Simmering Antagonisms between the Rival Tutsi and Hutu Tribes Explode into Violence," *New York Times Magazine,* November 6, 1988, 90–99, 125.

country's president on this question. According to the *Washington Post,* "Buyoya said the soldiers who killed Hutu civilians were not acting under government orders but started the slaughter after discovering the bodies of Tutsi tribesmen."[2] There was a third question, never resolved, about the number of victims.

The *New York Times* on August 23 reported a Burundi government claim that its army showed remarkable restraint. In its August 22 briefing, the government reported that at least five thousand people had been killed in ethnic clashes that began with a Hutu attack on Tutsi. According to the *Times,* those at the briefing "generally interpreted the official acknowledgement of 5,000 dead as a sign that the Government was eager to avoid a cover-up similar to that in massacres in 1972." The government apparently never raised that estimate, which was based on counts by grave-diggers, though Burundi's president later hinted that the number might be higher. Dr. Ralph Dupré, a German surgeon who treated people wounded in the massacres, estimated the dead at twenty thousand. Newspaper reports attributed similar estimates to unnamed church and medical workers, diplomats, and refugees. A high estimate by a diplomat quoted in the *New York Times Magazine* was fifty thousand killed. Frequently cited estimates of the number of refugees in Rwanda were fifty to sixty thousand.[3]

The government of Burundi turned aside any suggestion of an outside investigation, saying that it was an internal matter. As a gesture of conciliation, President Buyoya appointed a Hutu prime minister, but the government attempted to deny the problem by claiming that ethnic distinctions did not exist.

2. "Burundi Leader Concedes Troops Killed Civilians," *Washington Post,* August 26, 1988, A18.

3. "Burundi Reports 5,000 Are Dead in Resurgence of Tribal Warfare; Army Puts Down Strife, Said to Begin with a Hutu Attack on Tutsi," *New York Times,* August 23, 1988, 1; "Burundi Leader Tells of Army Reprisals," *Los Angeles Times,* August 26, 1988, 11; "Alive in a Wounded Nation: Burundi Survivors Recall Killing Frenzy," *Washington Post,* August 29, 1988, A1; "Burundi Leader Briefs Neighboring Leaders on August Hutu Massacres," *Los Angeles Times,* October 9, 1988, 6, pt. 2; "The Bloody Hills of Burundi," *New York Times Magazine,* November 6, 1988, 90–91.

The U.S. Congress passed a nonbinding resolution threatening to cut off aid unless the violence was stopped and ethnic inequality remedied. On September 8, the *Washington Post* reported a State Department announcement that the Reagan administration was not considering any cuts in economic aid to Burundi. Spokesman Charles Redman said, "It is clear to us that the government forces committed atrocities against civilians, and we condemn this. We also note that Burundi's president, Maj. Pierre Buyoya, has permitted journalists and embassy observers free access to the affected areas. We continue to seek first-hand information on what actually happened. We have also urged the Burundi government to accept international involvement in an inquiry into the causes of and solutions to the violence that periodically plagues the country."[4]

This was the last article in the twenty-day spurt of coverage that began on August 20. In the next two months there were a few briefs, editorials, letters to the editor, Perlez's magazine piece, and a *Post* article on the changes in the Burundi government. Then Burundi returned to its previous obscurity. The story of the massacres stayed on the news pages a little less than three weeks.

IRAQ'S POISON GAS ATTACKS ON NATIVE KURDS

On September 1, 1988, the *New York Times* reported a "drive to crush Kurds," with claims by Kurdish leaders and unnamed U.S. officials that Iraq was using chemical weapons against the Kurds (see figs. 7.2 and 7.3). Two Kurdish leaders were quoted as alleging "genocide" against their people. Turkish prime minister Turgut Ozal said that 20,000 Kurdish refugees had fled to Turkey, and Kurdish representatives said that as many as 100,000 were trying to flee because of fighting.[5] The reports garnered immediate credibility because of previous widely believed reports that Iraq had used mustard

4. "U.S. to Continue Aid to Burundi; State Department Plans No Changes Despite Tribal Massacre," *Washington Post,* September 8, 1988, A2.

5. "Iraq Reportedly Mounts a Drive to Crush Kurds; Gas Is Used in Assault, Protest to U.N. Says," *New York Times,* September 1, 1988, 1.

and nerve gas in early 1988 against Kurdish rebels and civilians, killing, the U.S. State Department said, as many as 2,000 people in the
Kurdish city of Halabja.[6] According to the *New York Times:*

> Since 1984, when it first started using chemical weapons, Iraq has de-
> ployed mustard gas or hyperite, which burns and blisters the skin and black-
> ens the flesh on contact, especially on parts of the body that are moist. The
> gas has a similar effect on the lungs if it is inhaled and can cause death. . . .
> To a lesser extent, Iraq has used Tabun, a . . . nerve gas developed by the
> Germans that causes convulsions, foaming and bleeding at the mouth, and
> often death.

In addition, photos from Halabja show the bodies of people believed to
have been subjected to gas attacks with bluish faces, a symptom associated
with cyanide gas that deprives the blood of oxygen and can cause death.

Although Iraq has been the primary user of chemical weapons, Western

Figure 7.2. Iraq, gas attacks, and the Kurds: A pattern of coverage by five
major newspapers, January 1988–March 1989

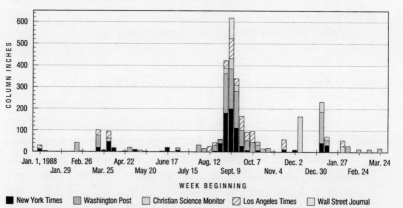

Note: Each bar represents a week. Newspaper coverage peaked in September 1988. For a detailed look at that period,
see figure 7.3. An international chemical weapons conference took place in January 1989.

6. Ibid.; "Rights Group Reports Iraq Poisoned Kurds" (Amnesty International); *New York Times,* January 13, 1988, 3; "Gas Attack Envelops Iraqi Town in
Cloud of Death; Killing of Kurds Blamed on Baghdad," *Los Angeles Times,* March 24,
1988, 1; "Poison Gas Attack Kills Hundreds; Iran Accuses Iraq of Atrocity in Kurdish Region Near Border," *Washington Post,* March 24, 1988, 1.

intelligence sources say there is some evidence that Iran may have been responsible for what appeared to be cyanide gas in the Halabja area.[7]

When the Iran-Iraq War was raging in early 1988, Amnesty International and the Iranian government sought to prompt a widespread outcry against Iraq's use of poison gas. The Iranian mission to the United Nations presented a thirty-five minute videotape of an alleged March 18 gas attack whose victims were mainly Kurdish civilians. According to the *Christian Science Monitor*, "First the film showed Iranian forces entering and touring a city. Then, in scenes filmed from a distance, explosions spread huge white clouds of gas

Figure 7.3. Iraq, gas attacks, and the Kurds: A pattern of coverage by five major newspapers, August 24–October 16, 1988

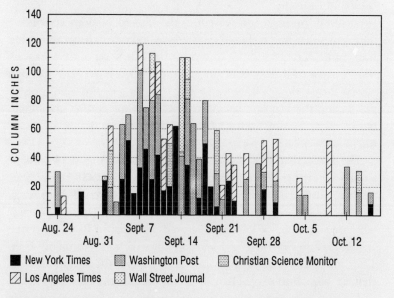

Note: Each bar represents a day. Coverage peaked during first three weeks of September.

7. "Shultz to Question Iraqi Official Today on Reported Gas Use against Kurds," *New York Times*, September 8, 1988, 6.

over whole sections of the city. Finally the film showed another tour of the city, with corpses of civilians everywhere." According to the *Monitor,* Iranian officials said that five thousand were killed and seven thousand wounded by Iraqi chemical weapons, and an organization of doctors, the Médecins sans Frontières, confirmed at least two thousand killed and five thousand wounded. On the evening of March 22, American television showed scores of dead Iraqi Kurds in Halabja. White House spokesman Marlin Fitzwater told reporters, "Everyone in the administration saw the same reports you saw last night. They were horrible, outrageous, disgusting and should serve as a reminder to all countries of why chemical warfare should be banned." The potentially galvanizing effect of video had been demonstrated in October 1984, when NBC broadcast a BBC report of famine in Ethiopia.[8]

In 1988, prior to the cease-fire, the United Nations concluded three times that Iraq had used mustard gas and other chemicals against Iran, commenting in the third report that Iraq's use of the weapons was "intense and frequent." In August the U.N. Security Council passed Resolution 620, condemning Iraq for illegally using poison gas during the war and asking the secretary-general to investigate future allegations by Security Council members on the use of chemical or bacteriological weapons.[9]

The attacks that were reported to have begun on August 24 brought a change in the tone and quantity of coverage. In 1988 before September, headlines mentioning Kurds frequently descried them as aggressors or combatants, "rebels" who "clash with Turkish troops," who are suspected of killing a German diplomat in Paris, who free Italian hostages in Iraq, and who, as allies of Iran, "torment" Iraq. Thus it appears that in this case, as in others, the mass killing of civilians was camouflaged by war. It may be that the Kurdish victims

8. Robert D. Kaplan, *Surrender or Starve: The Wars behind the Famine* (Boulder, Colo.: Westview Press, 1988), 37–38.
9. "U.S. and Allies Ask U.N. to Send Team to Kurdish Areas; Inquiry on Gas Use; Specific Evidence of Chemical Warfare Would Be Sought—Access Is Uncertain," *New York Times,* September 13, 1988, 1.

of Iraqi gas attacks were seen before September as casualties of war, victims of a distant and anomalous revival of a First World War horror weapon. Moreover, some of the most substantial evidence of atrocity—the videotape and the marshaling of victims—came from the despised Iranian government, not the most credible witness in the court of Western public opinion. (A U.S. Defense Department study released in May 1990 suggests that Iran pressed its accusations in order to cover its own use of cyanide.) [10]

But on August 20, 1988, a cease-fire ended the Iran-Iraq War. New Kurdish victims of gas attacks clearly were not casualties of an international war, and though some headlines mentioned Kurdish "rebels," the Kurds were more often characterized as refugees, victims of an "onslaught," an "assault," a drive to "crush" them, a "massacre." At the beginning of September, the reports of chemical attacks ballooned into a major story and remained one for about three weeks. By September 5 the columnists and editorial writers had begun speaking out. William Safire of the *New York Times* called the events "a classic example of genocide" and compared Iraq's Saddam Hussein to Pol Pot and Idi Amin. Safire asserted, "The world's film crews are too comfortable in Israel's West Bank, covering a made-for-TV uprising of a new 'people,' to bother with the genocidal campaign against a well-defined ethnic group that has been friendless throughout modern history and does not yet understand the publicity business." Other opinion writers were similarly outspoken. [11]

10. "Both Iraq and Iran Gassed Kurds in War, U.S. Analysis Finds," *Washington Post,* May 3, 1990, A37.

11. William Safire, "Stop the Iraqi Murder of the Kurds," *New York Times,* September 5, 1988; "What the Flag Can't Hide," *New York Times,* September 5, 1988, editorial about persecution of Hutu in Burundi and Kurds in Iraq; Vera Beaudin Saeedpour, "Wars against the Kurds Never Become World's Issue," *Los Angeles Times,* September 7, 1988; Richard Cohen, "And Iraq Keeps Spreading Its Poison Gas," *Washington Post,* September 7, 1988; "Gassing the Kurds," *Washington Post,* September 8, 1988, editorial; Jim Hoagland, "Make No Mistake—This Is Genocide," *Washington Post,* September 8, 1988; "Saddam Hussein's Vengeance," *Wall Street Journal,* September 9, 1988, editorial; "Hardly a Peep on Poison Gas," *New York Times,* September 10, 1988, editorial; "Stopping the Horror," *Los Angeles Times,* September 12, 1988, editorial.

But even while many opinion writers were expressing outrage, others were beginning to introduce doubt and ambiguity. On September 10, the *New York Times* published two articles together—"Turkey Asserts Iraq Has Ended Offensive in Kurdish Region," and on September 12, "Doctor Expresses Doubt on Kurds; Turk Links Symptoms to Diet and Health in Remote Area." And on September 15 the *Christian Science Monitor* packed all the ambiguity into a short headline, itself so contradictory as to defy comprehension: "Kurds Show Signs, Little Evidence, That Iraq Used Chemical Weapons."

The evidence was weakened by reporters' apparent inability to assimilate massive anecdotal evidence from refugees into any sort of reliable, conclusive report. Reporters' skepticism was very likely compounded by an episode in Afghanistan, Laos, and Cambodia, where alleged "yellow rain" poison gas attacks by the Soviets turned out, experts concluded later, to be bee feces, to which a naturally occurring poisonous fungus occasionally attached itself. Secretary of State Alexander Haig, seeking a propaganda club with which to bash the Soviets, ignored the warnings of his own experts in bringing the initial 1981 charge on the basis of very little evidence. Later anecdotal evidence from numerous refugees was based on minimal medical evidence and haphazard interviewing techniques involving leading questions and contamination of testimony by rumors among the refugees. Rigorous interviewing techniques, combined with other investigative rigor, would have prevented this fiasco.[12]

In the Iraqi case, similarly rigorous interviewing techniques, including the isolation, correlation, and cross-checking of testimony, would have strengthened the claim, perhaps conclusively, that poison gas attacks had taken place. On-site checking for poison residue in Iraq was at first impossible, and the medical evidence, doctors said, was inconclusive. Doctors examined refugees and found symptoms consistent with poison gas, but were unable to assert that tear gas or some other cause did not produce the symptoms. But to con-

12. "U.S. Reports Disputed 'Yellow Rain' Charges," *Washington Post*, August 30, 1987, A1; "U.S. 'Yellow Rain' Reports Rebutted," *Washington Post*, May 29, 1986, A1.

clude otherwise required discounting the eyewitness testimony of the refugees.

The doubts were compounded by Iraqi denials and Turkish ambivalence about the influx of Kurdish refugees with their tales and symptoms of gassing. Turkey, with its own sometimes restive 8.5 million Kurds (called "mountain Turks" in an attempt at assimilation), wanted to be seen as a democratic, humane European power but without alienating its neighbor to the south.

In a refugee camp, a Turkish government physician examined thirteen-year-old Bashir Semsettin. A reporter observed that the boy's "chest and upper back had been seriously burned in a marbled pattern, with deep brown streaks of skin—so dark they were almost black—surrounding patches of pink. His chest hurt, he said. He had frequent instances of runny nose. He had been fine, Bashir said, until eight Iraqi planes dropped poisonous gas on the village of Warmil." [13] The Turkish doctor said, "I know these are first-degree burns from a heat source other than flames. If they were flames, his hair and eyebrows would also be burned. But I can't say if they're from chemicals. They can be from anything." And the chief physician of the Diyarbakir camp, working under the auspices of the Turkish Red Crescent, described skin blistering and the camp's nearly epidemic eye problems—itching, watering, blurring—as the result of "malnutrition, and improper medical care and poor cleanliness." [14]

There was a variety of evidence that the Kurds were suffering from more than poor sanitation. Their own testimony was consistent, the *Christian Science Monitor* reported. "The attacks started early on Aug. 24, the refugees say, with the arrival of Iraqi aircraft. They released bombs that didn't detonate as usual. Instead, they delivered a yellow vapor, described as smelling sweet or pungent, like fermented wheat. The clouds were choking, the refugees say, and death came quickly to those who breathed in the vapors. The people fell to

13. "Poison-Gas Use or Not, a Trauma for the Kurds," *New York Times,* September 13, 1988, 4.
14. "Doctor Expresses Doubts on Kurds: Turk Links Symptoms to Diet and Health in Remote Area," *New York Times,* September 12, 1988, 1.

the ground or, if they were sleeping, did not wake up. Afterward, their bodies turned blue."[15]

Further evidence lay in the unprecedented exodus of tens of thousands of Iraqi Kurds, including guerrillas who said they were not afraid of Iraqi planes and guns but were afraid of poison gas. "Evidently, something has scared them, but what's scared them to this point of mass exodus I can't say," said a Turkish cabinet member.[16] And one *New York Times* writer concluded, "It is believed that Washington . . . relied on other intelligence sources for its indictment of Iraq because it considered the evidence [at the Diyarbakir camp] damning but not conclusive."[17]

According to Milton Viorst, writing in the opinion section of the *Washington Post,* the State Department's evidence, chiefly radio intercepts, was not made available to U.S. allies because it "may be subject to conflicting interpretations." Viorst's conclusion after visiting Iraq was that Iraq "probably used gas—of some kind—in air attacks on rebel positions. . . . But doctors sent by France, the United Nations and the Red Cross have said these symptoms could have been produced by a powerful tear gas, a conventional weapon (alas!) in today's warfare. None would assert that the gas was lethal."[18]

Two weeks after the first reports, the Iraqi government allowed reporters to visit Kurdish areas near the Turkish border in an orchestrated tour designed to show reporters for themselves that there had been no use of chemical weapons. The reporters knew they could not, on such a tour, determine whether gas had been used, but they were out to see what they could learn. The tour was a public relations failure for Iraq. Reporters saw a truck full of soldiers wearing gas masks; they saw two hundred Kurds who had supposedly returned from Turkey under an amnesty program, except they had

15. "Verifying Kurdish Claims: Kurds Show Signs, Little Evidence, That Iraq Used Chemical Weapons," *Christian Science Monitor,* September 15, 1988, 8.

16. Ibid.

17. "Poison-Gas Use or Not, a Trauma for the Kurds," *New York Times,* September 13, 1988, 4.

18. "Poison Gas and 'Genocide': The Shaky Case against Iraq," *Washington Post,* October 5, 1988, A25.

never been to Turkey; later the journalists were taken to the Turkish border to photograph returning Kurds, but none showed up; and when the tour was over, Iraq seized all videotapes and refused to transmit a *New York Times* story. A brigadier general on the scene denied using chemical weapons in the August action, but said, "If those Khomeini guards want to come and take over our land, we can use any weapons we want to drive them out." In the Kurdish cities the reporters saw relaxed civilians and children who seemed unafraid of the soldiers, and they constantly heard Kurdish people sing songs in praise of Saddam Hussein, subject of a major personality cult. But they saw something more grim as they flew over in a government helicopter—an entire valley, ten miles wide, scorched and depopulated, its villages destroyed. In all, diplomats supposed, hundreds of villages were razed, bombed, or burned out. The Iraqi government admitted for the first time that it had for two years been working to relocate a large population of Kurds, out of the mountain villages and away from the border areas, into modern compounds with electricity and running water, where they could be controlled, where they would not have contact with their relatives in Turkey and Iran, and where they would not trouble the government or the city-dwelling Kurds.[19] (Because many modern cases of genocide have involved forcible relocation—the Holocaust, the Armenians, the Ukraine, Cambodia, Ethiopia, Paraguay, to name some important examples—this massive and brutal relocation of Kurds inside Iraq should be followed closely by those concerned with preventing genocide.)

A week after the flyover, Patrick E. Tyler, the *Washington Post's* chief Middle East correspondent, concluded in a commentary piece:

Genocide, the extermination of a race of people and their culture, . . . is not an accurate term for what is happening in [the Kurdish] part of Iraq. But something horrible and historic is indeed being wrought. . . .

19. "Kurds Disappoint Iraqi PR Effort; Reporters Taken to Border to See Returnees, But None Show," *Washington Post*, September 18, 1988, A30; "Scorched Kurdish Villages Bear Witness to Iraqi Assault; Valley Was Targeted for Relocation Drive," *Washington Post*, September 17, 1988, A1; "Kurds Can't Go Home Again, Because the Homes Are Gone," *New York Times*, September 18, 1988.

Life is changing here drastically for the Kurds under a massive and forced relocation program that was accelerated two years ago to break the centuries-old cycle of trouble between rebellious mountain Kurds and town-dwelling Kurds who cooperate with the government. Baghdad is bent not only on depopulating the region but on closing its borders in the high mountains, cutting off Iraqi Kurds from brothers, sisters, cousins in Turkey and Iran. . . .

The major towns and cities of Kurdistan are still standing unscathed and populated by Kurds who cling to their rich culture under the protection of a government that recognizes some amount of Kurdish autonomy and condones and encourages the preservation of the Kurdish way of life.

Tyler said that the city-dwelling Kurds were never the targets of the Iraqi action but noted that the relocation program would "drastically" change the culture of Kurdistan, "which has always been marked by open lines of communication across international borders." Tyler wrote that in August Iraqi troops may have hoped to execute a pincer movement to seal the northern border and then sweep up from the south to surround and wipe out the twenty thousand rebel fighters. A Western ambassador in Baghdad said, "If they had successfully kept them [the refugees] in Iraq, they could have done what they like without the world knowing it." But their massive flight set off by gassing and the ensuing panic triggered alarms in Western governments and human rights organizations, and one observer said, "The Iraqis were forced to stop that action."[20]

After the flyover reports, the story began winding down. The fate of the refugees was reported: Iran agreed to accept 100,000 in the spring; in Turkey they moved into concrete winter houses. The newspapers covered deliberations over proposed U.S. sanctions against Iraq, which were supported unanimously in the Senate, watered down in the House, opposed by the White House, and finally allowed to die in Congress. The Reagan administration opposed sanctions because it saw them as disrupting its diplomatic objectives in the Middle East. Instead, it sought to focus on reaffirming the international norm against chemical warfare, and to that end, President Ronald Reagan,

20. Patrick E. Tyler, "The Kurds: It's Not Genocide, But Iraq's Policy of Repression and Relocation Is Still Horrific," *Washington Post*, September 25, 1988, C5.

in September 1988, proposed an international conference to strengthen the 1925 convention against chemical and biological warfare. In January 1989 Kurds demanded that the conference, to be held in Paris, focus on the Iraqi attacks. The sanctions would not have taken effect anyway because of a loophole—the president could lift them if Iraq agreed not to use chemical weapons and the president was able to certify compliance. Iraq did promise not to use the weapons.[21]

On December 4, the *New York Times* published a story headlined "Traces of Chemical Indicated Iraq Used Gas against Kurds." But the world had not needed to wait to find out whether gas had been used. Only by disbelieving or ignoring the testimony of refugees had it been possible to doubt what had happened.

REBEL ATROCITIES IN MOZAMBIQUE

A massive exodus of refugees from Mozambique, which was expected to pass the million mark by the end of 1988, prompted a State Department investigation. The State Department consultant, Robert Gersony, interviewed 200 refugees, selected to obtain a representative cross section. He found they were fleeing violence of the Mozambican National Resistance (known as RENAMO, an acronym for the Portuguese name, Resistensia Nacional Moçambican), an insurgent organization seeking to overthrow the government of Mozambique. Some 170 of those who fled in 1987–1988 reported "about 600 murders by RENAMO of unarmed civilians, in the absence of resistance." The investigator concluded that if the accounts were accurate and the sample representative, it was "conservatively estimated that 100,000 civilians may have been murdered by RENAMO." The 170 refugees also reported "many hundreds of cases of systematic forced portering, beating, rape, looting, burning of villages, abductions and mutilations" throughout Mozambique.[22]

21. "U.S. Debates Sanctions against Iraq," *Christian Science Monitor,* October 14, 1988, 8.

22. Robert Gersony, "Summary of Mozambican Refugee Accounts of Principally

Newspaper articles mentioning Mozambique came in clusters throughout the fifteen-month period, dropping very low in the last quarter of 1988 (see fig. 7.4). Most of the headlines related in some way to the civil war there and the associated suffering. The headlines however, varied over time in how they tended to characterize the conflict and RENAMO. In the months before the State Department report was issued on April 20, there were seven headlines mentioning RENAMO; three characterized the group or its actions in a neutral way, three negatively, and one a mixture of negative (allegedly derailing a train and killing twenty-two) and perhaps positive, at least as many U.S. readers would construe it ("guerrillas opposed to Marxist rule"). Headlines negatively portrayed the rebels as "reportedly" using "thousands" of kidnapped children as soldiers, making attacks that "batter food relief efforts," and receiving backing from South Africa.

Figure 7.4. Insurgent atrocities in Mozambique's civil war: A pattern of coverage by five major newspapers, January 1988–March 1989

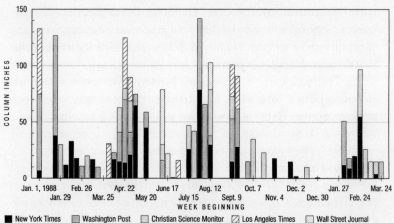

Note: Each bar represents a week. Newspaper coverage of Mozambique's civil war came in spurts.

Conflict-Related Experience in Mozambique," report submitted to U.S. State Department, April 1988, 41–42.

Before the State Department report there were eleven headlines mentioning the conflict. They tended to characterize the war as disrupting food aid and causing human suffering, but except for the report of RENAMO's impressing of child soldiers, the headline reader might easily take away the impression that there was a civil conflict with hapless civilians caught in the middle. During that period there were no headlines portraying RENAMO as a vicious perpetrator of atrocities, three characterizing the war as interfering with food aid, and none mentioning refugees. There were four mentions of South Africa, but only one suggesting South African support for RENAMO.

But with the release of the State Department report came a cluster of headlines with a new and highly negative characterization of REN-AMO. They spoke of rebels' "brutality," of "slaughter" and "war atrocities." A "visiting U.S. aide" condemned the rebels, and Jesse Jackson, then a presidential candidate, raised the war as a campaign issue by supporting military aid for the embattled government of Mozambique. Some headlines that did not mention the perpetrators nonetheless raised an alarm. A headline for a *New York Times* editorial, "Killing Fields of Mozambique,"[23] invoked a phrase used as the title of a movie depicting Khmer Rouge atrocities, which is gaining standing as a term for mass killing. And a *Washington Post* column's headline cried out, " 'Massive Evil' in Mozambique: 'Children Die Every Day So That Apartheid May Live.' "[24] For the first time in the period under discussion, the headlines began mentioning refugees. And some depicted South Africa as the behind-the-scenes perpetrator: "Pretoria's Victims in Mozambique."[25]

Within two weeks of the report even South Africa was apparently trying to distance itself from RENAMO, and on May 5 the *New York Times* reported, "South Africa Apparently Shifting Loyalty to Support Mozambique." Some fourteen subsequent headlines in this study

23. "Killing Fields of Mozambique," *New York Times,* April 23, 1988, 14(N), 30(L).
24. Kevin Lowther and C. Payne Lucas, *Washington Post,* April 27, 1988, 21. The quotations in the headline are extracts from the article itself, an op-ed piece written by two development officials.
25. *Washington Post,* April 28, 1988, A22.

mentioned South Africa. Nine characterized Pretoria as conciliatory, seeking rapprochement with Mozambique's government or an end to the war. Two depicted South Africa as hostile, and three were neutral in their characterizations. The rulers of South Africa and Mozambique, P. W. Botha and Joachim Chissano, met in September to renew a 1984 agreement not to support guerrilla wars against each other, and this meeting accounted for three of the conciliatory characterizations.

In September a visit to Mozambique by the pope generated eight headlines. Four had him urging peace but did not quote him as deploring atrocities or pointing a finger of blame. By the time of the pope's and Botha's visits to Mozambique, about five months had passed since the issuance of the State Department paper.

In late July RENAMO invited some journalists to fly to a secret base inside Mozambique, a move characterized by the *Washington Post* as an "Attack on the PR Front." The effort resulted in several lengthy articles, skeptical in tone, that quoted the RENAMO leaders' denials of atrocities.[26]

Subsequently, the tone of headline coverage drifted away from mention of atrocities or highly negative characterization of RENAMO. One headline said "US Discredits Renamo Rebels"; another cited reports that rebels "Specifically Target Schools and Towns for Violent Attack," and they were called a "Hazard" on the "Road to Prosperity." Otherwise the most negative mention was, "Rebels Said to Kill 31 in Raid."[27] Although Mozambique's war stayed in the news, the image of RENAMO as a perpetrator of atrocities faded from the headlines, and the emphasis was more on a war-torn nation, with a crippled economy, a suffering population, and a shattered infrastructure.

26. "Mozambican Guerrillas Launch Attack on the PR Front," *Washington Post*, July 31, 1988, A1; "Pariahs Abroad, Mozambique Rebels Fight On," *New York Times*, July 31, 1988, 1.
27. "Rebels Said to Kill 31 in Raid," *New York Times*, December 4, 1988, 9.

CONCLUSION

In each of the cases described, the party accused of atrocities sought to defend itself—Burundi by blaming "invading rebels from Rwanda" or "exiled dissidents"; Iraq by denying it had gassed the Kurdish civilians, by giving a tour to journalists, and by pledging not to use chemical weapons; RENAMO by hosting a visit by journalists and by claiming the atrocities were invented by enemies or committed by governments out to make RENAMO look bad.

Burundi largely succeeded in its apparent public relations goals; there were no sanctions or U.N. investigations, and Burundi dropped from the news, returning to its accustomed obscurity.

Iraq succeeded in part: sanctions were avoided, the truce with Iran did not collapse, and the opprobrium of having used gas over a four-year period was largely lifted and diffused in a larger discussion of banning chemical and biological weapons worldwide. The newspaper accounts of Iraq's gassing Kurds did not precisely vanish; it is more as if the focus was changed to chemical warfare rather than the killing of the victims. Other villains arose—Libya as well as German companies accused of supplying Libya with materials and technology to make poison gas weapons. But the sort of rapprochement with the West that Iraq had hoped would come with peace was postponed as governments kept their distance.

(After Iraq's invasion of Kuwait in August 1990, it was hard to find skeptics about Iraq's past record of gas attacks. During the Gulf War in early 1991, civilians and soldiers in Israel and Saudi Arabia responded to each Scud missile attack as if it might be a gas attack, putting on gas masks that were generally distributed. In explaining these fears, reporters sometimes mentioned Saddam Hussein's prior gas attacks on the Kurds, or "on his own people.") [28]

28. Whatever Saddam's reasons for not, apparently, launching gas attacks against Israel or Saudi Arabia in early 1991, newspaper reports after the cease-fire suggested that he had not forsworn the use of gas warfare under all circumstances. Marines returning to the United States said they had been targets of an Iraqi chemical weapons attack in Kuwait on the second day of the ground offensive, but that wind and the

In the case of RENAMO, the "atrocity" characterizations prompted by the April 1988 State Department report eventually faded even as coverage of the civil war continued. Leaders of RENAMO were concerned that international support from right wingers was drying up after all the bad publicity. South Africa's uneasy efforts to distance itself from the rebel group did nothing to bolster RENAMO's standing. But a headline in the February 25, 1989, *New York Times* stated, "New Mozambique Violence Is Blamed on South Africa."

These three cases, like almost all large-scale atrocities, had in common a massive outflowing of refugees. In each case it was the refugees who brought the problem strongly into the world spotlight and transformed the claims of atrocities into an international issue. Until refugees find a permanent home, they are a burden on neighboring countries, a source of information about the worst side of life in the country they have fled, and an occasion for embassy visitors, U.N. inquiries, and heartrending film images. As long as there are refugees, abuses cannot be credibly described as a purely domestic issue.

Journalists should be skeptical, but skepticism is best expressed through careful investigation, not by presenting speculation about factual matters that can be resolved. Refugee testimony, the most extensive source of eyewitness accounts in the early stages of large-scale atrocities, has not been fully exploited as a source by newspapers. Rather, the papers in this study presented refugee testimony in

---

small amount of gas made the attack ineffective. Military officials in the United States expressed skepticism. On February 24 a U.S. general said marines detected a "wee little bit" of gas about ten miles inside Kuwait, apparently released by buried mines. More ominously, on March 2 (according to the *Los Angeles Times*) the *New York Times* reported that Iraqi officials had authorized using chemical weapons against antigovernment rebels, and the Bush administration had warned Iraq not to do it. A Shiite Muslim opposition leader accused Saddam of using mustard gas, heavy artillery, and helicopter gunships against rebels and said casualties numbered in the hundreds. And on March 4 U.S. military officials in Iraq, near the Kuwaiti border, issued a chemical weapons alert after a report that chemical weapons may have been used by both Iraq's Republican Guard and the insurrectionists in Basra. ("Returning Marines Say They Were Targets of Gas Attack," Associated Press, March 12, 1991; " 'Saddam Line' Falls Easily to Marines," *Los Angeles Times*, February 25, 1991, 1A; "Hussein Forces Counterattack in Basra; Many Flee Fighting," *Los Angeles Times*, March 6, 1991, 1A; "2 More American POWs Freed; Iraq Beset by Turmoil," March 9, 1991, 1A.)

an anecdotal fashion and quoted speculation from noneyewitness official sources about what really happened. Sophisticated survey methods, which were applied daily, expensively, and redundantly to predict the outcome of the U.S. presidential elections, could have been used by the media to understand what was happening in Iraq. Tens of thousands of refugees were available to be interviewed. Jason Clay of Cultural Survival and other scholars have developed such techniques for painting a picture of civil conflict by interviewing refugees, cross-checking their stories, and using statistical methods to project the results onto a larger population. It should be possible for a media pool to fly in a trained team of interviewers, spend days interviewing refugees, and come up with an authoritative conclusion about what is happening inside a country.

Newspaper articles are complex messages. The initial sender may be a government or refugee spokesman who calls in the press to convey a point of view. But the intended message is modified by the reporter's own observations and by the practice of getting other viewpoints—not just getting "both sides" but also consulting with presumably disinterested observers, such as embassy people, relief workers, and so on. Sophisticated reporters are aware that a speaker's position and point of view will influence the reader's interpretation of what is said, and they therefore try to characterize the speaker precisely in a few words—for example, "a senior Western diplomat who attended the briefing today."

The reporter's observations can have a powerful effect in modifying or blotting out a speaker's intended message. An example is the account of the Turkish government doctor who observed burns on a Kurdish teenager and said it was impossible to say what caused the burns. The reporter's description of the symptoms and of the youth's own story conveyed to readers that what caused the dreadful marbled burns on the boy's skin was very likely a chemical weapon. Again, the Iraqi government, flying reporters over Kurdistan, apparently was so inured to the Kurdish suffering and devastation that they did not realize the impact of allowing reporters to describe or photographers to picture the dozens of razed, bombed, and burned-out villages. The Iraqi army lost control of the message and, by seizing film and attempting to censor a reporter's dispatch, revealed that—too late—they realized their mistake.

But if the reporter's observations and interviews cast doubt on the statements of propagandists, the quoting of diverse viewpoints and the quest for objectivity can also cause readers to doubt what really happened. As one Amnesty International activist lamented to me, with so many bad things in the world to worry about, how much time will a reader have to be outraged about a merely "alleged" atrocity? If the propagandist's goal is to dampen outrage and prevent intervention, it may be sufficient to sow doubt and keep ambiguity alive.

Journalists realize this and have various ways of breaking free of the fuzzifying conventions of newswriting. Reporters on the scene may write an "analysis," dropping the pretense of objectivity and saying what they think really happened. Columns and editorials can also express openly the writer's point of view.

This is not to say that ambiguity should be dropped from news reporting. Where uncertainty exists, good reporting will convey that uncertainty. But the best reporting will seek aggressively to get beyond the uncertainty as quickly and as accurately as possible. Learning to gather and evaluate the statements of refugees may prove to be a key to reporting on atrocities and genocide.

James E. Mace   *Chapter 8*

THE AMERICAN PRESS AND
THE UKRAINIAN FAMINE

AUTHOR'S NOTE: During my studies in history at the University of Michigan, I wrote a doctoral dissertation on Ukrainian communism—later published as *Communism and the Dilemmas of National Liberation* (Cambridge: Harvard University Press, 1983)—and became aware of how Ukrainian cultural and political life was virtually extinguished by the famine of 1933. Later, I worked with Robert Conquest in researching *Harvest of Sorrow* (New York: Oxford University Press, 1986), which documents the Ukrainian famine. Between 1986 and 1990, I served as staff director of the U.S. Government Commission on the Ukraine Famine, whose report to Congress determined that the famine was an act of genocide for which Stalin was directly responsible.

   In 1932–1933 several million Soviet citizens, most of them Ukrainians, starved to death in a famine organized by Joseph Stalin and his closest collaborators. In brief outline, what happened was this: at the end of 1929, Stalin decreed a crash policy of forced collectivization throughout the Soviet Union. As a result, agricultural production declined precipitously. In the spring of 1930 and again in early 1932, he decreed temporary measures to ameliorate the situation, even sanctioning food aid for peasants east of the Volga River in 1932. But he abruptly reversed course that summer when he was warned of impending mass starvation in the Ukrainian republic and the North Caucasus territory, areas that constituted the main stumbling blocks to the centralization of political and administrative authority in his hands. He ordered a campaign of grain seizures, sanctioning a level of force unparalleled even in the history of Stalinism: everything that could be eaten was taken from those who had produced it. At the same time, the relative autonomy Ukrainians had hitherto enjoyed was suppressed, and every manifestation of Ukrainian cultural distinctiveness was condemned as "bourgeois nationalism."[1]

All the while, the authorities completely denied their activities and lauded the happy life in the Soviet countryside. Even starving peasant children were told by their schoolteachers that any mention of the everyday reality of the starvation around them was "anti-Soviet" propaganda; they were taught to sing "Thank You, Comrade Stalin, for a Happy Childhood."[2] At home and abroad, Stalin made every attempt to conceal the famine and to deny those reports that managed to surface. In this he was aided by a number of prominent Moscow correspondents for American newspapers.

1. See, e.g., Robert Conquest, *The Harvest of Sorrow: Soviet Collectivization and the Terror-Famine* (New York: Oxford University Press, 1986); Commission on the Ukraine Famine, *Investigation of the Ukrainian Famine, 1932–1933: Report to Congress* (Washington: U.S. Government Printing Office, 1988); Roman Serbyn and Bohdan Krawchenko, eds., *Famine in Ukraine, 1932–1933* (Edmonton: Canadian Institute of Ukrainian Studies, 1986); James E. Mace, "The Man-Made Famine of 1933 in Soviet Ukraine," in *Toward the Understanding and Prevention of Genocide: Proceedings of the International Conference on the Holocaust and Genocide,* ed. Israel Charny (Boulder, Colo.: Westview Press, 1984), 67–83; James E. Mace, "Famine and Nationalism in Soviet Ukraine," *Problems of Communism,* May-June 1984, 37–50; James E. Mace, "The Politics of Famine: American Government and Press Response to the Ukrainian Famine, 1932–1933," *Holocaust and Genocide Studies* 3, no. 1 (April 1988): 75–94.

2. James E. Mace and Leonid Heretz, eds., *Investigation of the Ukrainian Famine, 1932–1933: Oral History Project of the Commission on the Ukraine Famine* (Washington: U.S. Government Printing Office, 1990), I: 407; II: 607.

The story broke in March 1933 when Gareth Jones, a British student of Russian history and former aide to David Lloyd George, returned from an unauthorized trip to Ukraine. He declared: "I walked alone through villages and twelve collective farms. Everywhere was the cry, 'There is no bread; we are dying.' " He also estimated that a million people had perished in Kazakhstan since 1930, a number that now seems conservative, and that in Ukraine millions more were threatened.[3] Eugene Lyons, at the time the United Press Moscow correspondent, called this the first reliable press report published in the English-speaking world.[4]

Another British correspondent reported the famine at about the same time as Jones. Malcolm Muggeridge recalled that the famine "was the big story in all our talks in Moscow. Everybody knew about it. . . . Anyone you were talking to knew that there was a terrible famine going on. . . . I could see that all the correspondents in Moscow were distorting it. Without making any kind of plans or asking for permission, I just went and got a ticket for Kiev and then went on to Rostov. . . . Ukraine was starving, and you only had to venture out to smaller places to see derelict fields and abandoned villages."[5] Muggeridge's unsigned account, published in the *Manchester Guardian* at the end of March, stated that in both Ukraine and the North Caucasus, "it was the same story—cattle and horses dead; fields neglected; meagre harvest despite moderately good climatic conditions; all the grain that was produced taken by the Government; now no bread at all, no bread anywhere, nothing much else either: despair and bewilderment."[6] In another, signed article published in May, after he left the Soviet Union, he wrote:

3. "Famine in Russia, An Englishman's Story: What He Saw on a Walking Tour," *Manchester Guardian,* March 30, 1933, 12.

4. Eugene Lyons, *Assignment in Utopia* (New York: Harcourt Brace, 1937), 572.

5. Marco Carynnyk, "Malcolm Muggeridge on Stalin's Famine: 'Deliberate' and 'Diabolical' Starvation," in *The Great Famine in Ukraine: The Unknown Holocaust* (Jersey City: Ukrainian National Association, 1983), 47.

6. "The Soviet and the Peasantry: An Observer's Notes. II. Hunger in the Ukraine," *Manchester Guardian,* March 27, 1933, 10.

On a recent visit to the North Caucasus and Ukraine, I saw something of the battle that is going on between the Government and their peasants. The battlefield was as desolate as in any war, and stretches wider. . . . On one side, millions of peasants, starving, often their bodies swollen with lack of food; on the other, soldiers, members of the GPU, carrying out the instruction of the dictatorship of the proletariat. They had gone over the country like a swarm of locusts and taken away everything edible; they had shot and exiled thousands of peasants, sometimes whole villages; they had reduced some of the most fertile land in the world to a melancholy desert.[7]

William Henry Chamberlin, the initially pro-Soviet Moscow correspondent of the *Christian Science Monitor,* had reported as early as July 1933 that though there was no actual starvation in Moscow, "Grim stories of out-and-out hunger come from southern and southeastern Russia, from the Ukraine, the North Caucasus and from Kazakhstan, where the nomadic natives seem to have suffered very much as a result of the wholesale perishing of their livestock."[8] In April 1934, after leaving the Soviet Union, he published an article in *Foreign Affairs,* confirming yet again that the famine had taken place and giving ample "refutation of the idea that as a result of collectivization, Russian agriculture will leap forward."[9] In May Chamberlin reported that during the preceding year "more than 4 million peasants are found to have perished."[10] In his book *Russia's Iron Age,* published in October, he estimated the death toll as a direct result of the famine of 1932–1933 to be not less than 10 percent of the population of the areas affected, according to the local officials with whom he had spoken.[11]

7. Malcolm Muggeridge, "The Soviet's War on the Peasants," *Fortnightly Review* 39 (May 1933): 564.

8. W. H. Chamberlin, "Rations Given U.S. Jobless Enough for Soviet Official, Amazed Russian Workers Say," *Christian Science Monitor,* July 3, 1933, 1.

9. W. H. Chamberlin, "Ordeal of the Russian Peasantry," *Foreign Affairs,* April 1934, 506.

10. W. H. Chamberlin, "Famine Proves Potent Weapon in Soviet Policy," *Christian Science Monitor,* May 29, 1934, 1. Second of thirteen articles serialized under the heading "Russia without Benefit of Censor," May 28–June 18, 1935.

11. W. H. Chamberlin, *Russia's Iron Age* (Boston: Little Brown, 1934), 367–368.

Yet, despite these and other accounts, the famine story was quickly contained. Ignored at the time it took place, the famine was so quickly forgotten that it ranks as history's most successful instance of the denial of genocide by the perpetrators. The United Press Moscow correspondent at the time of the famine, Eugene Lyons, wrote in 1937, "Years after the event, when no Russian Communist in his senses any longer concealed the magnitude of the famine—the question whether there had been a famine at all was still being disputed in the outside world."[12]

DILUTING THE FACTS WITH EUPHEMISM

The initial containment of the story is perhaps the crucial event in what Lyons called "the whole shabby episode of our failure to report honestly the gruesome Russian famine of 1932–33."[13] Jones had based his account not only on visits to twenty villages but also on what he had been told by diplomats and other Western correspondents in Moscow.[14] Diplomats, however, were forbidden to publish their observations, and the journalists were circumspect because they had much to lose, including their visas.[15]

12. Lyons, *Assignment in Utopia*, 577–578.
13. Ibid., 572.
14. Ibid., p. 575; Gareth Jones, "Mr. Jones Replies: Former Secretary of Lloyd George Tells of Observations in Russia," *New York Times*, May 13, 1933, 12.
15. For example, in January 1933, Ralph Barnes reported to the old *New York Herald Tribune* from the then Ukrainian capital of Kharkiv, a place under the watchful eye of the Soviet censor but also one in which the famine was already painfully evident. Barnes wrote not about what he must have seen but rather about the officially acknowledged "abuses" of the previous year: "Grain needed by the Ukrainian peasants as provisions was stripped from the land a year ago by grain collectors desirous of making a good showing. The temporary or permanent migration of great masses which followed alone prevented real famine conditions. All those persons with whom I have talked, in both town and village, agree that the food situation in this vast area is worse than it was last year. It is inconceivable, though, that the authorities will let the bread shortage on the collective farms reach a stage comparable to that of the late winter and spring of last year." Ralph W. Barnes, "Grain Shortage in the Ukraine Results in Admitted Failure of the Soviet Agricultural Plan," *New York Herald Tribune*, January 15, 1933, sec. II, p. 5. By contrast, a Ukrainian who arrived in Kharkiv

In dealing with foreign correspondents, the Soviet authorities held the trumps. Correspondents lived in the Soviet Union at the government's sufferance and could be expelled at any time. They had to submit their stories to censorship before the state-owned telegraph agency would send them out. Jones could not have cabled his story from Moscow; he spoke out only after leaving. Had Muggeridge signed his stories in the *Manchester Guardian,* which were sent by British diplomatic pouch, he would have been summarily expelled. Correspondents also depended on the authorities for access to the news on which their jobs depended. News is, after all, a competitive business, and the state could always see to it that correspondents were singly or collectively admitted or denied access to news.

Immediately after the Jones and Muggeridge stories appeared, Moscow responded by forbidding journalists to travel to famine-stricken areas, thereby denying them direct access to the story.[16] At the same time, the Soviet authorities blatantly used another story to which the state controlled access, a show trial of British engineers employed by the Metropolitan Vickers Corporation. When Jones

---

the preceding month, i.e., at least two weeks before the above story was filed, later recalled that at the time of his arrival the railroad station was already crowded by starving beggars, and the dead and dying were already being loaded into freight cars to be transported outside the city. Oleksa Hay-Holowko, "The World Should Be Made Aware of Its Greatest Tragedy," *Ukrainian-Canadian Review,* February 1985, 24.

16. Lyons recalled: "We were summoned to the Press Department one by one and instructed not to venture out of Moscow without submitting a detailed itinerary and having it officially sanctioned. In effect, therefore, we were summarily deprived of the right of unhampered travel in the country to which we were accredited.

" 'This is nothing new,' Umansky grimaced uncomfortably. 'Such a rule has been in existence since the beginning of the revolution. Now we have decided to enforce it.'

"New or old, such a rule had not been invoked since the civil war days. It was forgotten again when the famine was ended. Its undisguised purpose was to keep us out of the stricken regions. The same department which daily issued denials of the famine now acted to prevent us from seeing it with our own eyes. Our brief cables about this desperate measure of concealment were published, if at all, in some obscure corner of the paper. The world press accepted with complete equanimity the virtual expulsion of all its representatives from all of Russia except Moscow. It agreed without protest to a partnership in the macabre hoax." Lyons, *Assignment in Utopia,* 576.

broke the story of the famine, Lyons recalled how the matter was settled in cooperation with Konstantin Umansky, the Soviet censor-in-chief:

We all received urgent queries from our home offices on the subject. But the inquiries coincided with preparations under way for the trial of the British engineers. The need to remain on friendly terms with the censors at least for the duration of the trial was for all of us a compelling professional necessity.

Throwing down Jones was as unpleasant a chore as fell to any of us in years of juggling the facts to please dictatorial regimes—but throw him down we did, unanimously and in almost identical formulas of equivocation. . . . The scene in which the American press corps combined to repudiate Jones is fresh in my mind. It was in the evening and Comrade Umansky, the soul of graciousness, consented to meet us in the hotel room of a correspondent. He knew he had a strategic advantage over us because of the Metro-Vickers story. He could afford to be gracious. Forced by competitive journalism to jockey for the inside track with officials, it would have been professional suicide to make an issue of the famine at this particular time. There was much bargaining in a spirit of gentlemanly give-and-take, under the effulgence of Umansky's gilded smile, before a formula of denial was worked out.

We admitted enough to soothe our consciences, but in round-about phrases that damned Jones as a liar. The filthy business having been disposed of, someone ordered vodka and *zakuski,* Umansky joined in the celebration, and the party did not break up until the early morning hours.[17]

When Jones replied to his most energetic attacker, Walter Duranty of the *New York Times,* he rightly took to task those journalists whom "the censorship has turned . . . into masters of euphemism and understatement." They gave "famine the polite name of 'food shortage' and 'starving to death' is softened down to read as 'widespread mortality from diseases due to malnutrition,' "[18] This use of euphemism and of "softening down" the truth allowed the journalists to compromise without losing self-respect, for they could always tell themselves that they had told all they could have and still con-

17. Ibid., 575–576.
18. Gareth Jones, "Mr. Jones Replies," *New York Times,* May 13, 1933, 12.

tinue to report from the country to which they were accredited. Besides, the journalist could tell himself, the astute reader could read between the lines. Isn't that what Western journalists themselves did in order to penetrate the codes of official Soviet press? Perhaps some of them became so used to reading between the lines that they forgot that their readers had not necessarily acquired the same skill.

OUTRIGHT DENIAL

Despite mounting and increasingly irrefutable evidence that famine was raging in Ukraine, two American correspondents in Moscow, Walter Duranty of the *New York Times* and Louis Fischer of the *Nation,* took the lead in publicly denying its existence.

Duranty, the most famous correspondent of his day and the dean of the American press corps in Moscow, won a Pulitzer Prize in 1932 for "dispatches . . . marked by scholarship, profundity, impartiality, sound judgement and exceptional clarity . . . excellent examples of the best type of foreign correspondence."[19] When read with the benefit of hindsight, his stories are a wonderful example of pseudo-objectivity—of explaining things the way his readers wanted to believe they were rather than as they really were. In the words of James Crowl, "What is so remarkable about Duranty's selection for the Pulitzer is that, for a decade, his reports had been slanted and distorted in a way that made a mockery of the award citation. Probably without parallel in the history of these prestigious prizes, the 1932 award went to a man whose reports concealed or disguised the conditions they claimed to reveal, and who may even have been paid by the Soviets for his deceptions."[20]

The charge that Duranty was on Stalin's payroll has never been—

19. Quoted in James William Crowl, *Angels in Stalin's Paradise: Western Reporters in Soviet Russia, 1917 to 1937: A Case Study of Louis Fischer and Walter Duranty* (Washington: University Press of America, 1982), 143.

20. Ibid. A second major study of Duranty reaching basically the same conclusion is S. J. Taylor, *Stalin's Apologist: Walter Duranty, the New York Times's Man in Moscow* (New York: Oxford University Press, 1990). Unfortunately it was received too late to be used adequately in this chapter.

and probably never will be—proved. What we can prove is that—whether compensated in cash or in some other way—he was virtually a public relations man for Stalin. In 1931, on one of his trips outside the Soviet Union, Duranty had a conversation with A. W. Kliefoth of the American embassy in Berlin. The memorandum of this conversation, now declassified, states, "Duranty pointed out that, 'in agreement with the *New York Times* and the Soviet authorities,' his official dispatches always reflect the official opinion of the Soviet regime and not his own."[21] Given Duranty's record of mendacity, this is slim evidence on which to convict the *Times* for anything more than gullibility and incompetence. But it is as good as a signed confession for Duranty.

In 1932, as the situation in Ukraine and the North Caucasus went from bad to worse, Duranty's attitude initially vacillated. At first he viewed the developing crisis in foodstuffs with considerable alarm, hoping that Stalin would offer further concessions to complement those made during the first half of 1932—a modest reduction in grain quotas and a promise that peasants would ultimately be able to keep something and sell it after meeting state procurements.

In late fall, however, it became clear that there would be no further concessions, and Duranty began to minimize and explain away difficulties as "growing pains," the results of peasant lethargy in some districts and the "marked fall in the living standards of a large number of peasants." By mid-November he stressed that there was "neither famine nor hunger." Although there were "embarrassing" problems, they were not "disastrous." Two days later he wrote that though there might be "an element of truth" in reports of a food shortage, the problem was "not alarming much less desperate." He suggested that Soviets might not eat as well as in the past, but "there is no famine or actual starvation, nor is there likely to be." "The food shortage," Duranty took pains to explain on November 26, "must be regarded as a result of peasant resistance to rural socialization."

21. A. W. Kliefoth, U.S. Embassy, Berlin, "Memorandum, June 4, 1931," 2; 861.5017-Living Conditions/268; T1249; Records of the Department of State; National Archives, Washington D.C.

The situation would not have been serious if world food prices had not fallen, "which forced the Soviet Union to increase the expropriation of foodstuffs at a time when the shoe was beginning to pinch and the distribution of the food at home would have corrected many difficulties." Still, he concluded, "it is a mistake to exaggerate the gravity of the situation. The Russians have tightened their belts before to a far greater extent than is likely to be needed this winter." Even the *New York Times* editorialized on November 30 that collectivization was nothing but "a ghastly failure." As if in reply, Duranty reported that the Soviets could always release stockpiled grain if the problem became more acute.[22]

Next to Duranty, the American reporter most consistently willing to gloss Soviet reality was Louis Fischer, who had a deep ideological commitment to Soviet communism dating back to 1920.[23] But when he traveled to Ukraine in October and November of 1932 he was alarmed by what he saw. "In the Poltava, Vinnitsa, Podolsk, and Kiev regions, conditions will be hard," he wrote. "I think there is no starvation anywhere in Ukraine now—after all, they have just gathered in the harvest—but it was a bad harvest."[24] Initially critical of the Soviet grain procurement program because it created the food problem, Fischer by February had adopted the official Stalinist view, blaming the problem on Ukrainian counterrevolutionary nationalist "wreckers." It seemed that "whole villages" had been contaminated by such men, who had to be deported to "lumbering camps and mining areas in distant agricultural areas which are now just entering upon their pioneering stage." These steps were forced upon the Kremlin, Fischer wrote, but the Soviets were, nevertheless, learning how to rule wisely.[25]

Fischer was on a lecture tour in America when Gareth Jones's famine story broke. Asked about the million who had died since

22. J. W. Crowl, *Angels in Stalin's Paradise,* 150–152, 159.

23. Ibid., 22–25 and passim.

24. Louis Fischer, "Soviet Progress and Poverty," *Nation,* December 7, 1932, 553. Cited in Crowl, *Angels in Stalin's Paradise,* 153.

25. Idem., "Soviet Deportations," *Nation,* February 22, 1933, 39.

1930 in Kazakhstan, he scoffed, "Who counted them? How could anyone march through a country and count a million people? Of course people are hungry there—desperately hungry. Russia is turning over from agriculture to industrialism. It's like a man going into business on small capital."[26] Speaking to a college audience in Oakland, California, a week later, Fischer stated emphatically, "There is no starvation in Russia."[27]

The Jones story also caught Duranty by surprise. He claimed that Jones had concocted a "big scare story" based on a "hasty" and "inadequate" glimpse of the countryside consisting of a forty-mile walk through villages around Kharkiv. He went on to claim that he himself had made a thorough investigation and discovered no famine, although he did admit that the food shortage had become acute in Ukraine, the North Caucasus, and the Lower Volga Basin. This he attributed to mismanagement and recently executed "conspirators" in the Commissariat of Agriculture. Still, he wrote, "there is no actual starvation, but there is widespread mortality from diseases due to malnutrition." And the hardship was worth it: "To put it brutally, you can't make an omelette without breaking eggs."[28]

Only in August 1933, in the course of a story denouncing "exaggerated" émigré claims, did Duranty admit that "in some districts and among the large floating population of unskilled labor" there were "deaths and actual starvation."[29] Later that month, he reported that though the "excellent harvest" of 1933 had made any report of famine either "an exaggeration or malignant propaganda," there had been a "food shortage" that had caused a "heavy loss of life" in Ukraine, the North Caucasus, and Lower Volga Basin.[30] In September, Dur-

26. " 'New Deal' Needed for Entire World, Says Visiting Author," *Denver Post,* April 1, 1933, 3. Cited in Crowl, *Angels in Stalin's Paradise,* 157.

27. "Too Much Freedom Given to Russia's Women, Says Writer," *San Francisco News,* April 11, 1933, 2. Cited in Crowl, *Angels in Stalin's Paradise,* 157.

28. Walter Duranty, "Russians Hungry But Not Starving," *New York Times,* March 31, 1933, 13.

29. Walter Duranty, "Russian Emigres Push Fight on Reds," *New York Times,* August 13, 1933, 2.

30. Walter Duranty, "Famine Toll Heavy in Southern Russia," *New York Times,* August 24, 1933, 1.

anty was the first Western reporter allowed to go to Ukraine and the North Caucasus after the imposition of the ban on travel there by journalists. William Stoneman of the *Chicago Daily News* had managed to find a way to get to Ukraine without permission and had filed an accurate account, leading the Soviets to send their most favored journalist to sweeten the pill.[31] Now able to report truthfully a good harvest, Duranty also belatedly reported what he had known all along: "Hard conditions had decimated the peasantry. Some had fled. There were Ukrainian peasants begging in the streets of Moscow last winter, and other Ukrainians were seeking work or food, but principally food, from Rostov on Don to White Russia and from the Lower Volga to Samara."[32] In short, he admitted the truth only after others had done so more explicitly and always in a context designed to show his readers that things were not nearly so bad as other sources might indicate.

He was more explicit in private. In December 1932, he told an American diplomat in Paris that he was deeply pessimistic because of "the growing seriousness of the food shortage."[33] In September 1933, after returning from Ukraine and the North Caucasus, he talked with a British diplomat who reported to London, "Mr. Duranty thinks it quite possible that as many as 10 million people may have died directly or indirectly from lack of food in the Soviet Union during the past year."[34]

Eugene Lyons also recalled that at dinner with Duranty,

he gave us his fresh impressions in brutally frank terms and they added up to a picture of ghastly horror. His estimate of the dead from famine was the most startling I had as yet heard from anyone.

31. Joseph Alsop, *FDR, 1882–1945: A Centenary Remembrance* (New York: Viking, 1982), 249.

32. Walter Duranty, "Big Soviet Crop Follows Famine," *New York Times,* September 16, 1933.

33. U.S. Embassy, Paris, "Memorandum of Remark Made by Mr. Walter Duranty," December 8, 1932, 2; 861.5017-Living Conditions/752; T1249; Records of the Department of State; National Archives.

34. William Strang, British Embassy, Moscow, to Sir John Simon, September 30, 1933, republished in Marco Carynnyk, Lubomyr Luciuk, and Bohdan Kordan, eds., *The Foreign Office and the Famine: British Documents on Ukraine and the Great Famine of 1932–1933* (Kingston, Ontario: Limestone Press, 1988), 313.

"But, Walter, you don't mean that literally?" Mrs. McCormick exclaimed.

"Hell I don't. . . . I'm being conservative," he replied, and as if by way of consolation he added his famous truism: "But they're only Russians . . ."

Once more that same evening we heard Duranty make the same estimate. . . . When the issues of the *Times* carrying Duranty's own articles reached me I found that they failed to mention the large figures he had given freely and repeatedly to all of us.[35]

Muggeridge also provided a telling vignette of Duranty in 1933: "He'd been asked to write something about the food shortage, and was trying to put together a thousand words which, if the famine got worse and known outside Russia, would suggest that he'd fore-seen and foretold it, but which, if it got better and wasn't known outside Russia, would suggest that he'd pooh-poohed the possibility of there being a famine. He was a little gymnast. . . . He trod his tightrope daintily and charmingly."[36] Half a century later Mugger-idge put it less elegantly: "Duranty was the villain of the whole thing. . . . It is difficult for me to see how it could have been otherwise that in some sense he was not in the regime's power. He wrote things about the famine and the situation in Ukraine which were laughably wrong. There is no doubt whatever that the authorities could manip-ulate him."[37]

Duranty admitted, then denied, the famine to John Chamberlain, book critic for the *New York Times*. Chamberlain wrote in his auto-biography:

To a group in the *Times* elevator Duranty had almost casually mentioned that three million people had died in Russia in what amounted to a man-made famine. Duranty, who had floated the theory that revolutions were beyond moral judgement ("You can't make an omelet without breaking eggs."), did not condemn Stalin for the bloody elimination of the kulaks that had deprived the Russian countryside of necessary sustaining expertise. He just simply let the three-million figure go at that.

What struck me at the time was the double iniquity of Duranty's perfor-

35. Lyons, *Assignment in Utopia,* 580.
36. Malcolm Muggeridge, *Winter in Moscow* (Boston: Little, Brown, 1934), 162.
37. Interview with Bohdan Nahaylo, Robertsbridge, England, March 1, 1983.

mance. He was not only heartless about the famine, he had betrayed his calling as a journalist by failing to report it.[38]

On the basis of Duranty's remark, Chamberlain, hitherto a communist sympathizer, decided to review a book entitled *Escape from the Soviets*. Written by Tatiana Tchernavina, who had escaped via Finland, the book had earlier been rejected because it presented the Soviet Union in too negative a light. When Chamberlain, in his review, mentioned peasants starving, he was immediately attacked by the American communists and their sympathizers. Chamberlain recalled that then "Duranty, with his visa hanging fire, denied ever having said anything." With losing his job a distinct possibility, Chamberlain was saved by fellow book reviewer Simeon Strunsky, who testified that he had heard Duranty say the same thing.[39]

Meanwhile, Louis Fischer continued to deny the famine's existence and to extol the virtues of Soviet life. "The first half of 1933 was very difficult indeed," he admitted in August 1933. "Many people simply did not have sufficient nourishment. The 1932 harvest was bad, and to make matters worse, thousands of tons of grain rotted in the fields because the peasants refused to reap what they knew the government would confiscate under the guise of 'collection.' "[40] But Fischer, straining to justify the Soviet government, wrote in January 1934 that "during all those hard years . . . the state endeavored to beautify life. . . . The opera, the ballet, and many theaters displayed a dazzling richness of scene and costume incomparably greater than elsewhere in the world. Parks of culture and rest were established throughout the country to provide sensible recreation and civilized leisure." Fischer also adopted a line often used to justify evil: "All governments are based on force. The question is only of the degree of force, who administers it, and for what purpose. . . . Force which eliminates oppressors and exploiters, creates

38. John Chamberlain, *A Life with the Printed Word* (Chicago: Regnery Gateway, 1982), 54–55.

39. Ibid., 55.

40. Louis Fischer, "Russia's Last Hard Year," *Nation*, August 9, 1933, 154–155.

work and prosperity, and guarantees progress and economic security will not be resented by the great masses of people."[41]

William Randolph Hearst made a final attempt to use the famine to attack President Franklin D. Roosevelt. His newspaper chain ran a series of articles on the famine in 1935, in the style for which the term *yellow journalism* was coined. Written by Thomas Walker, the articles may have been a reworking of authentic material from 1933 that Hearst either bought or borrowed. Undoubtedly at Hearst's behest, Walker "updated" the story by placing the famine in 1934 rather than 1932–1933.[42] Fischer, who had been to Ukraine in 1934 and, of course, saw no famine, accused Walker of "inventing" a famine. He interpreted the whole affair as an attempt by Hearst to "spoil Soviet-American relations" as part of "an anti-red campaign."[43]

Fischer was challenged by W. H. Chamberlain, who wrote from Tokyo, chiding Fischer for his failure to mention that 1932–1933 had seen "one of the worst famines in history":

I feel justified in recalling my personal observations of this famine because, although it happened two years ago, I think it will probably still be "news" to readers of *The Nation* who depend on Mr. Fischer for their knowledge of Russian developments. I have searched brilliant articles on other phases of Soviet life for a single, forthright, unequivocal recognition of the famine although he was in Russia during the period of the famine and was scarcely ignorant of something that was common knowledge of Russians and foreigners in the country at the time.

Fischer responded that he had not been in the Soviet Union during the famine, that he had mentioned it in his book, *Soviet Journey*, but that he, unlike Chamberlain, did not put all the blame on the Soviet government.[44] In *Soviet Journey* he wrote: "History can be cruel. . . .

41. Louis Fischer, "Luxury in the U.S.S.R.," *Nation,* January 31, 1934, 120–121.

42. Serialized in five installments in the *New York Evening Journal,* February 19–27, 1935. See also *Chicago American,* March 1–6, 1935.

43. Louis Fischer, "Hearst's Russian 'Famine,'" *Nation,* March 13, 1935, 296–297.

44. *Nation,* May 29, 1935, 629.

The peasants wanted to destroy collectivization. The peasants used the best means at their disposal. The government used the best means at their disposal. The government won."[45]

Hearst, with Walker exposed as someone who had never gone near Ukraine, began in 1935 to publish true accounts that had been available for some time, but lacked some of Walker's journalistic aplomb. Harry Lang, who had earlier published an account of his 1933 journey to Ukraine in the *Jewish Daily Forward,* wrote a series that reported his being told by a Soviet official that 6 million had perished.[46] Richard Sanger, later a distinguished U.S. diplomat, had gone with his wife to the Soviet Union in 1933 and gave the figure of 4.5 million.[47]

Perhaps the most interesting of these accounts was that of Adam Tawdul, a Ukrainian-American whose family had known Ukrainian Communist strongman Mykola Skrypnyk in the Bolshevik underground before coming to the United States in 1913. Tawdul returned to Ukraine in 1931 and, thanks to this acquaintance, was able to move in high circles. Tawdul claimed that before Skrypnyk committed suicide in July 1933 he told him that 8 to 9 million had perished of starvation in Ukraine and the Caucasus, and that another official had told him an additional million or two had died in the Ural region, the Volga basin, and in western Siberia.[48]

As for those who denied outright the existence of the famine: Fischer, who broke with the Soviets following the Spanish civil war, later admitted that the Ukrainian famine had cost the lives of millions.[49] Looking back, he recalled that even then, "my own attitude

45. Cited by Eugene Lyons, *The Red Decade: The Stalinist Penetration of America* (Indianapolis: Bobbs-Merrill, 1941), 118.

46. *New York Evening Journal,* April 15–23, 1935. Lang's original account was published in the *Jewish Daily Forward* (Yiddish), December 27, 1933.

47. *New York Evening Journal,* April 29–March 9, 1935; on his subsequent career, see his obituary, *Washington Post,* March 30, 1979.

48. Adam J. Tawdul, "10,000,000 Starved in Russia in Two Years, Soviet Admits," *New York American,* August 18, 1935, 1–2; Adam J. Tawdul, "Russia Warred on Own People," *New York American,* August 19, 1935, 2. The Tawdul series continued until August 31.

49. In Richard Crossman, ed., *The God That Failed* (New York: Bantam, 1959), 188.

began to bother me. Was I not glorifying steel and kilowatts and forgetting the human being? All the shoes, schools, books, tractors, electric light, and subways in the world would not add up to the world of my dreams if the system that produced them was immoral and inhuman."[50]

Duranty, never an idealist like Fischer, could not be disillusioned because he had no illusions in the first place. In later years, when Sovietophilism had gone out of fashion, Duranty lied about ever having lied in the first place. In his last book, published in 1949, he wrote, "Whatever Stalin's apologists might say, 1932 was a year of famine," and he claimed that he had said so at the time.[51] As we have seen, he had, but not in his dispatches to the *New York Times*.

PERCEPTUAL BIAS

Leaders of "enlightened" public opinion in this country tended to believe the official Duranty, debunker of scare stories, rather than those whose veracity his private conversations confirmed. For example, writing in the *New Republic*, Joshua Kunitz, quoting Stalin almost verbatim, put the blame not on collectivization but on "the lack of revolutionary vigilance" against "kulaks" who had not yet been liquidated and the "selfishness, dishonesty, laziness, and irresponsibility" of the peasants.[52]

There can be little doubt that American journalists collaborated with the Soviets in covering up the famine. Duranty, who privately admitted his role as a semiofficial Soviet spokesman as early as 1931 and who after the famine told British diplomats that as many as 10

50. Ibid., 189.

51. Walter Duranty, *Stalin and Co.: The Politburo—The Men Who Run Russia* (New York: Sloane, 1949), 78.

52. *New Republic*, May 10, 1933, 360. Compare with Stalin's January 11, 1933, joint plenum speech, in which he blamed the difficulties in carrying out the procurements on two things: kulaks who had managed to enter the collective farms and were undermining them from within, and the alleged laxity of party officials who were allowing the collective farmers to set up "all kinds of reserves," who had not realized that the collective farmer was still at heart a petty bourgeois and that the collective farms themselves were full of hidden class enemies. I. V. Stalin, *Sochineniia* (Moscow: Gosizdat, 1946–1952), 13:216–233.

million might have perished, seems to have played an especially crucial role in America's extension of diplomatic recognition to the Soviet government in November 1933. It was with Duranty that FDR,
even as a candidate, first publicly broached the issue of recognition.[53]
Duranty seems to have been determined that American public opinion not be negatively influenced on the eve of Roosevelt's negotiations with the Soviets. He thought it imperative that the United
States and the USSR establish diplomatic relations, and the famine,
especially if it was the result of Stalin's malevolence, was a stumbling
block that had to be removed. His influence on Roosevelt's perception of the Soviet Union was profound. As Joseph Alsop wrote:

The authority on Soviet affairs was universally held to be the *New York Times*
correspondent in Moscow, Walter Duranty. . . . The nature of his reporting
can be gauged by what happened in the case of the dire Stalin-induced famine in the Ukraine in the early 1930s. . . . The Duranty cover-up, for that
was what it was, also continued thereafter; and no one of consequence told
the terrible truth.

This being the climate in the United States, Roosevelt and [Harry] Hop-
kins would have had to be very different men to make boldly informed
judgements of the Soviet system and Stalin's doings and purposes in defi-
ance of almost everyone else who was then thought to be enlightened.[54]

Yet Duranty was only an opportunist who took advantage of
something far more pervasive, a climate of opinion that made telling
the truth about Stalinism almost an offense against good taste in
"enlightened" circles. Eugene Lyons, who initially went to the Soviet Union with every intention of defending it, described the ambivalence felt by most Western observers of the day:

53. Already in July 1932, soon after winning the nomination, FDR had lunch
with Duranty, indicating that he was "contemplating, in the event of being elected, a
new policy toward the Soviets." His stand was not clear, but "the Governor's international advisers feel that the United States could profit by adopting an attitude different from that taken by the Republican administrations of the last decade. . . . The
Governor for some time has manifested deep interest in the Soviet's experiment and
today he spent several hours asking Walter Duranty . . . about his many years of
experience in Russia. 'I turned the tables,' said the Governor. 'I asked all the questions
this time. It was fascinating.' " *New York Times,* July 26, 1932.
54. Alsop, *FDR, 1882–1945: A Centenary Remembrance,* 249.

I returned to the United States in April, 1934. More sharply than ever before I faced the dilemma: to tell or not to tell.

By 1934 exaggerated faith in the Soviet experiment had become the intellectual fashion among the people for whose good opinion I cared most. It was clear to me what sort of account of Russia the intellectual elite preferred to hear.

The editors of a liberal weekly invited me to a staff luncheon. It would have been the polite and kindly thing to bolster up their eager misconceptions. I was given an opening to denounce books about Russia that had told too much. News had just come through that the G.P.U. had been converted into a Commissariat for Internal Affairs. By stretching my conscience, I might have assured them that a new era of liberalism had dawned under the Soviets. But the Ukrainian famine, the valuta horrors, the death decrees and heresy hunts still smarted in my memory. I alluded to a few of these things. A chill seemed to come over the luncheon; apparently I had committed the offense of puncturing noble illusions. The Olympian irony of the situation—I could not help thinking of it—was that these men, their exact kind, were being stamped out in the Soviet land like so many insects. They fitted perfectly into the category of prerevolutionary intellectuals, who must hide in the dark cracks, praying for only one boon—not to be noticed.

Other intellectuals were no less frightened of the truth. They asked questions about Russia and appeared horrified if I failed to give the prescribed answers. Indeed, it seemed to me that these men and women, insulted to the marrow by the iniquities of bourgeois society, were wiping out the insult Japanese fashion by committing intellectual hara-kiri. . . .

The desire to "belong," not to be a political dog in the manger, was a powerful inducement to silence, or at least to cautious understatement.[55]

Today even the perpetrator government recognizes the historicity of the famine of 1933, and in February 1990 the Central Committee of the Communist Party of Ukraine published a special statement, admitting that the famine was artificially brought about by Stalin and his close associates.[56] But the 1930s was a "Red Decade" for

55. Eugene Lyons, "To Tell or Not to Tell," *Harper's,* June 1935; reprinted in *American Views of Soviet Russia, 1917–1965,* ed. Peter G. Filene (Homewood, Ill.: Dorsey Press, 1968), 107–108.

56. "Povidomlennia TsK KPU," *Radians'ka Ukraïna,* February 7, 1990, 4. The

many "enlightened" Americans, immunized to unpleasant truths about Stalin and the system he was creating by the attractiveness of socialist ideals. Their vaccination was part fear of disillusionment and part fear of being cast in with the ignorant rabble who read the Hearst press rather than the *New York Times*. And so enlightened Americans all the way up to the president either refused to believe or turned a blind eye to the famine as they would later to the terror of 1937–1938. Perceptual selectivity based on political conviction, the confusion of fact and principle such that facts are rejected when inconvenient to one's political ideals, is as much with us now as it was then. When will we recognize that truly massive destruction is always accompanied by fervently held political ideals? After all, the Young Turks did it for the salvation of the Ottoman Empire, the Nazis for a new Germany and purified Aryan race, the Stalinists for a world without classes or exploitation. Ideals are no less fervently held for being wrong or perverted. But the dead are also no less dead.

Central Committee's statement has in turn made possible for the first time in the USSR the publication of serious historical work and previously unpublished archival documents, most notably the collection recently published by the former Ukrainian Institute of Party History. *Holod 1932–1933 rr.: Ochyma istorykiv, movoiu dokumentiv* (Politvydav Ukraïna: Kiev, 1990).

Part Three

APPROACHES TO PREVENTION AND PUNISHMENT

REFLECTIONS ON THE PREVENTION OF GENOCIDE

AUTHOR'S NOTE: The background to this paper is the anguish I experienced while living in the extreme racist society of South Africa, and the renewed hope inspired by the Gandhian nonviolent resistance movement in 1952. The collapse of that movement and the government's response in perfecting the instruments of oppression led to work on the conditions under which nonviolent resistance might be effective in transforming regimes of racist and ethnic oppression. This was followed by research into the reverse situation, the comparative study of conflicts resulting in extreme violence and in genocide.

Reflections on genocide are introduced in my books *Race, Class and Power* (London: Duckworth, 1974) and *The Pity of It All* (Minneapolis: University of Minnesota Press, 1977). *Genocide: Its Political Use in the Twentieth Century* (New Haven: Yale University Press, 1981) and *The Prevention of Genocide* (New Haven: Yale University Press, 1985) are entirely devoted to the subject. My major preoccupations at present relate to the possibilities of preventing genocide and to active campaigning against genocide and mass killing.

This chapter offers suggestions for the prevention of genocide. The first section is concerned with the setting of standards that might contribute to the prevention of genocide. The second deals with active campaigning, drawing in part on the experience of the organization International Alert against Genocide and Mass Killing. But before turning to the main argument, I need to comment briefly on my approach to the problems of prevention.

In any discussion of preventive action against genocide, one needs to define the restraints under which one acts and the assumptions that inform one's approach. Powerful nations have many possibilities for initiating preventive action (and also for promoting a genocidal process, as in Afghanistan and Mozambique), whereas scholarly and international nongovernmental organizations must seek a hearing as supplicants in the centers of power or as petitioners for a fleeting mention by an often capricious press or a telegraphic television program. It is from the perspective of scholars and of international nongovernmental organizations that I now offer these reflections on the possibilities for preventive action against genocide.

Among the major restraints on preventive action are the obstacles to modifying the structures of offending societies. Systematic discrimination, mounting repression, and escalating violence, which carry the threat of mass killing, are often perfectly clear to the outside observer, but he has no point of entry for reversing the process of polarization and restructuring the society. This is often overlooked.

When I was teaching in South Africa and apartheid was being systematically implemented, we would await visits from international human rights experts with eager anticipation that they would suggest strategies we had not explored. And, indeed, they invariably came with their panaceas, such as the establishment of interracial clubs or the promotion of integrated education. But what contribution could interracial clubs make to the dismantling of apartheid? And in any event, participation in these clubs had been made a criminal offense. As for integrated education, government policy was to reverse the liberalizing trend toward increasing integration by establishing a comprehensive system of racially and ethnically exclusive education.

By way of further example, consider some of the measures advocated in response to the recent reprisal massacres by the Tutsi ruling minority against the Hutu in the central African state of Burundi. Thus, a former American ambassador to Burundi recommended territorial separation, reflecting insensitivity to the extensive intermingling and intermarriage of the two groups. Nor was a proposal based on proportional representation very helpful, since the allocation of 80 percent of the positions of power to the Hutu majority would be equated by the Tutsi with Hutu domination and the threat of Tutsi annihilation.

The United Nations Universal Declaration of Human Rights, the covenants, conventions, and protocols, may be viewed as an attempt to restructure societies on a voluntaristic basis. It is difficult to know what contribution has been made to the amelioration of offensive rule by this vast outpouring of ethical norms and the ratification of numerous covenants. But some of the negative consequences are very clear. For many years, the preoccupation with ethical norms was associated with, or perhaps even a cover for, the neglect of practical measures against gross violations of human rights. And now these norms and ratified covenants seem to be honored more in the breach than the observance. Nevertheless, the debates in the Commission on Human Rights are informed by the exalted rhetoric of high ethical norms, which serve to camouflage the often naked pursuit of national self-interest. And the most strident, self-righteous, and vitriolic denunciations of human rights violations seem to emanate from countries with the most deplorable record for oppressive government and annihilatory violence.

We should bear in mind, however, that even when there is a fairly general consensus in the denunciation of a "pariah" state, there may be formidable obstacles to the restructuring of its institutions and policies. The racially oppressive policies of the South African government, for example, have been continuously on the agenda of the United Nations. Apartheid is the founding father, as it were, of a gigantic U.N. industry. There have been great floods of denunciatory rhetoric, and many forests have been annihilated in the preparation of reports and in the drafting of resolutions with their supporting documentation. These have certainly restrained some of the excesses of the apartheid government. But they have not been effective in modifying the basic structure of South African society. It is only now that apartheid begins to be dismantled, but this is appreciably the result of increasing African militancy and of social and economic change.

If there are all these difficulties in the restructuring of individual societies, how much more formidable are the obstacles to modifying worldwide economic and political processes and to establishing a new world order. Thus, in a recent volume on *Genocide and the Modern Age*, the editors emphasize that in the modern age it is harder to locate the intention to commit genocide at the societal level because of the anonymous and amorphous structural forces that dictate the character of our world.[1] And there can be no doubt that the present structure of international relations facilitates the crime of genocide by the primacy accorded to national self-interest, the protection extended to offending governments, and superpower rivalry and destructive intervention in the internal affairs of divided and other vulnerable societies. But how then are we to modify and transform these anonymous and amorphous worldwide structural forces and to create a new world order in time to respond to the many genocidal emergencies?

Quite apart from these restraints imposed by the intractability of the external situation, we need to make certain assumptions as to the efficacy of different approaches to preventive action. In the first place, we must guard against the illusion that moral considerations will prevail in the circles of power, without, however, totally excluding the possibility that in certain circumstances they might contribute a supportive argument. Then, too, we must guard against the resort to meaningless surrogates for action or placebos. An approach is made to a member of parliament or a senator, who expresses sympathetic understanding through an aide and will see what can be done. Or a nongovernmental organization presents a submission to

1. Isidor Walliman and Michael N. Dobkowski, *Genocide and the Modern Age* (New York: Greenwood Press, 1987), xvi.

the U.N. Commission on Human Rights and leaves with a sense of accomplishment—or more realistically with the hope that perhaps something may come of it. But the probability is that these representations will have little or no effect unless they are part of an informed campaign of systematic action.

In this respect the campaign of the Bahá'ís against their persecution by the Iranian government is a model of informed and sustained action. Representations to their own governments by dedicated Bahá'í communities in different parts of the world lent support to the campaigns in the intergovernmental organizations, and as a result the Bahá'í international community was able to secure the active involvement of European states, both within the European Community and in the United Nations. In 1980 and 1981 the European Parliament passed unanimous resolutions condemning the persecutions and calling on the foreign ministers of the member states of the European Community to make representations to the Iranian government.

In the United Nations, the Bahá'í representatives sedulously avoided charges of genocide, following advice that the response would be recoil and avoidance, not sympathetic involvement. The submissions were always restrained, concentrating on the more acceptable charges of violations of human rights, systematic discrimination, and religious persecution. They were preceded by effective lobbying, so that the Bahá'í representatives were reasonably assured before entering the debating chambers that their proposals would receive majority support. And in 1982 the U.N. Commission on Human Rights passed a resolution requesting the secretary-general to establish direct contact with the Iranian government and to continue his efforts to ensure that the Bahá'í were guaranteed full enjoyment of their human rights. The international surveillance initiated by the Bahá'ís would seem to have restrained the large-scale massacres that earlier appeared imminent.[2]

In the case of the Bahá'ís, the action component was specifically

2. See Kuper, *The Prevention of Genocide* (New Haven: Yale University Press, 1985), 152–153 and 163–164.

focused on gross violations of the rights of the Bahá'ís in a particular country. At a more general level, there is the possibility of institutionalizing an action component related to a worldwide problem and providing for continuous monitoring and response and surveillance. In this connection, an important initiative was taken in the United Nations by the Anti-Slavery Society, which proposed that a standing committee of experts on slavery be set up to supervise application of the convention on slavery and recommend measures for its abolition. The society argued cogently for the establishment of permanent supervisory machinery to be manned by independent experts as essential for effective action against slavery. And after some twenty-five years of repetitive and tortuous and evasive verbiage, a U.N. working group on slavery was finally appointed.

The experience of this group would seem to support the contention of the Anti-Slavery Society that supervisory machinery was necessary for effective action against slavery. Certainly, there has been a change in the nature of the violations reported in the years since the establishment of the group and in its current preoccupations. This is reflected in a recommendation by the group at its meeting in 1987 that its name be changed from the "Working Group on Slavery and Slavery-like Practices" to a name more consonant with, and more descriptive of, its actual interests—namely, exploitation of sex, debt bondage, sale of children, and apartheid. Such a name might be the "Working Group on Contemporary Forms of Slavery."[3] Of course, this change could be a response to changes in social and economic conditions and in international relations, not significantly attributable to the supervisory machinery of the Working Group. There can be no doubt, however, that its example and activities have stimulated the establishment of other action-oriented working groups in the United Nations and that it has contributed to the setting of standards in the fields of its interest.

I now turn to my main argument, beginning with standard set-

3. United Nations E/CN.4/Sub 2/1987/25, 26.

ting as a contribution to the prevention of genocide, preparatory to considering the possibilities for active campaigning.

STANDARD SETTING

There are two doctrines in which standards have crystallized that are inimical to preventive action against genocide. These relate to humanitarian intervention and to self-determination.

Michael Bazyler, in a recent discussion of humanitarian intervention, defines the doctrine as the recognition of the "right of one nation to use force against another nation for the purpose of protecting the inhabitants of that other nation from inhuman treatment by the governing sovereign." He goes on to say that "because of real and imagined abuses the doctrine of humanitarian interventions has been disfavored in the post World War II era."[4]

The first potential abuse derives from the disparity in power between the parties. Since forceful intervention could mean exposure to the hazards of a costly and destructive war, the doctrine is likely to be invoked only against a relatively weak and vulnerable society, a situation all too reminiscent of colonial interventions. Then, too, there is the possibility, perhaps even the probability, that naked self-interest may masquerade as altruistic concern; at any rate, even under the most favorable circumstances, there is likely to be an infusion of self-interest. The result then could be the sacrifice of vulnerable societies to their more powerful neighbors, pursuing expansionist goals under the guise of dedicated service to humanity.

It should be borne in mind, however, that some of the past interventions, which could have been justified on humanitarian grounds, such as the intervention of India against Pakistan in support of the Bengalis and of Tanzania in Uganda under Idi Amin's regime, did not involve a great disparity in military power. Moreover, if the cri-

4. "Re-examining the Doctrine of Humanitarian Intervention in the Light of Atrocities in Kampuchea and Ethiopia," *Stanford Journal of International Law,* Summer, 1987, 548.

terion of purity of motive is to be applied, then many, perhaps most, of the interventions of the United Nations against gross violations of human rights would be invalidated and rejected. It would seem more appropriate, then, to judge each case on its merits, with a realistic acceptance of the impurity of motivations.

Nevertheless, it is clear that application of the doctrine readily lends itself to abuse and that the prerequisites for the exercise of the rights to humanitarian intervention need to be carefully specified, with concern for restraints against abuse. Bazyler, in his article, suggests the following criteria:

(a) the perpetuation of large-scale atrocities in the offending society;
(b) overriding humanitarian motives—the predominance of humanitarian concern over other motives;
(c) a preference for joint action, on the assumption that this would generally restrain invocation of the doctrine purely or predominantly for motives of self-interest, though not necessarily excluding this possibility; and
(d) the exhaustion of other remedies where feasible.[5]

But even compliance with these prerequisites is hardly a guarantee against abuses of the right of humanitarian intervention. Certainly joint action may simply lead to an overwhelming disparity of power deployed against a relatively weak and vulnerable state; and the predominance of humanitarian motivation is not readily established prior to the intervention. But leaving this aside, if one examines some of the recent interventions, the defeat of the Khmer Rouge by an invading Vietnamese army was surely to be preferred to the continuation of the Pol Pot regime, whatever the motivation, as was the intervention of the Indian army in Bangladesh. Both certainly performed a humanitarian service.

A further consideration is that under present conditions, there is almost invariably outside intervention in the internal affairs of weaker states. This may take the form of fomenting internal division or supporting one of the contending parties in the internal conflicts of a

5. Ibid., 598–607.

plural or divided society, or it may consist more simply in the exploitation of opportunities for profiteering from the sale of arms. In a situation, then, in which interventions motivated by self-interest are almost a routine of international relations, there is a much stronger argument for reinstatement of the right to humanitarian intervention.

In this discussion, I have assumed that international laws and norms are a significant element in international relations. But often, as one listens to debates in the United Nations, for example, it is difficult to resist the conclusion that these laws and norms are appreciably the rhetoric through which national self-interest is pursued. This is very apparent in discussion of the right to self-determination. One would expect the representative of the government of Cyrpus to assert and emphasize that "any action aimed at the partial or total disruption or impairment of the territorial integrity or political unity of an independent and sovereign state under the pretext of exercising a so-called right to self-determination was regarded as illegal and incompatible with the purposes and principles of the Charter of the United Nations and the norms of international law."[6] The assumption of political unity in contemporary Cyprus is certainly surprising. But leaving this aside, it is the oppressed peoples in these independent states who are likely to assert their right to self-determination, not the privileged rulers.

Self-determination in its original conception was a liberating, revolutionary ideology, and it has served this function, and continues to do so, in the decolonizing process. It is still invoked against contemporary colonization, as by Indonesia in East Timor. It is also invoked against military interventions, such as the Vietnamese invasion of Kampuchea, the Russian intervention in Afghanistan, and the U.S. support for the contras in Nicaragua. And it remains a radical revolutionary ideology for third world countries in extending the free determination of political status to include also economic, social, and cultural sovereignty.[7] For the rest, the doctrine has been

6. See his submission, United Nations, E/CN.4/1987/SR.13, para. 24.
7. See my discussion of these issues in chap. 5 of *Prevention of Genocide*.

domesticated to serve the interests of ruling classes, most notably in U.N. practice.

The ideological transformation consists in viewing self-determination as inapplicable to the internal relations of peoples within an independent state. And since many of the independent states in the contemporary world are divided societies, characterized by conflicts between the different peoples they comprise, the result is the exclusion of a doctrine that could contribute to a process of conciliation. The exclusion is reinforced by a tendency to equate self-determination with secession, which appears to be anathema to the rulers of plural (or divided) societies.

The encouragement or acceptance of secession would, of course, be very threatening. One recalls the warning given by the Pakistani ambassador to the United Nations when his country was confronted by the secessionary movement in East Pakistan (Bangladesh): "The fragmentation that it symbolizes can occur in Europe, Asia, Africa and Latin America, and it cannot leave untouched the Great Powers themselves—in Uzbekistan and other parts of the world. There will not be a Bangladesh only in Pakistan: There will be a Bangladesh everywhere. . . . Let us open the floodgates, because if sovereign states are going to be mutated in this fashion, let the deluge come."[8]

Part of the problem is a contradiction between basic principles of international relations, as formulated in the United Nations. On the one hand, there is a strong affirmation of the right to self-determination, expressed in the most positive and comprehensive terms and accorded pride of place in both the International Covenant on Economic, Social and Cultural Rights, and the International Covenant on Civil and Political Rights. It reads as follows:

Article 1. All peoples have the right to self-determination; by virtue of that right they freely determine their political status and freely pursue their economic, social, and cultural development.

On the other hand, there is an injunction against impairment of the territorial integrity or political unity of sovereign states, which con-

8. United Nations, S/PV 1611, p. 21.

flicts with the free exercise of the right of self-determination. However, there is a proviso to this protection, which tends to be conveniently ignored. The authoritative General Assembly Declaration on Principles of International Law concerning Friendly Relations and Cooperation among States in accordance with the Charter of the United Nations[9] formulates the protection accorded states and the proviso to it in the following terms:

Nothing in the foregoing paragraphs shall be construed as authorizing or encouraging any action which would dismember or impair, totally or in part, the territorial integrity or political unity of sovereign and independent states conducting themselves in compliance with the principle of equal rights and self-determination of peoples as described above and thus possessed of a government representing the whole people belonging to the territory without distinction as to race, creed or color.

The Declaration on Principles of International Law then reconciles the protection of sovereign states against impairment of their political unity and territorial integrity with the preservation of the right to self-determination in situations where the government does not respect the equal rights of people or represent the whole people without distinction as to race, creed, or color. And it is precisely in situations of discrimination and oppression that the right to self-determination is likely to be invoked.

There is such a frenzied reaction to demands for separation (pejoratively described as secession) that it can probably be achieved only by civil war or powerful international intervention. But in most cases it is preceded by quite moderate demands for reform or a greater measure of autonomy. There is usually a long process of petitions, which are ignored or result in quite derisory reforms, or the promise, or indeed legislation, of significant reforms, which are not implemented. The movement for separation becomes the culmination of many years of contemptuous frustration of legitimate demands. This process may be traced, for example, in Algeria prior to the civil war against the French and in Sri Lanka since independence.

9. See G.A. Resolution 2625 (XXV), dated October 24, 1970.

It is particularly in the early stages of movements for greater equality in human rights, or some form of autonomy, that a more liberal approach to self-determination could contribute to peaceful reconciliation and release the productive energies of divided societies. A vast thesaurus of constitutional solutions is available, with many skilled practitioners in the arts of constitutional reform, whose services I am sure would be offered freely.

Fortunately, reaffirmation of self-determination as a right available to abused ethnic, racial, and religious groups within a sovereign state can proceed outside the United Nations, which is a most unlikely forum for this purpose. It is, after all, an organization of ruling groups, inevitably conservative and protective of the interests of its members, with a frequent tendency to gravitate, in practice if not in rhetoric, to the lowest common denominator.

However, I do not want to minimize the actual or potential contribution of the United Nations. Where there is operative implementing machinery, it can certainly make a contribution. Then, too, it offers a forum for alerting international opinion. In some situations, advisory services are available. There is usually assistance for refugees and the occasional availability of peacekeeping forces. But in cases of gross violations of human rights, the United Nations must usually be activated by outside organizations and by skillfully planned and coordinated representations. And given the U.N. structure and its record on gross violations of human rights and genocide, there is certainly a need for an independent basis of action.

This calls for an effective educational program to convey knowledge of past genocides in their different manifestations and the continuing contemporary incidence of the crime and also, one hopes, to encourage concern for, and a commitment to, preventive action.

CAMPAIGNING AGAINST GENOCIDE

There are at present ethnic and religious organizations engaged in teaching about their own particular genocide. This can be inclusive, extending sympathy to other groups, or it can be exclusive and alienating.

Quite apart from these genocide-specific programs, there are now institutes concerned with genocide in general. And there are curricula in some school systems concerned broadly with the protection of human rights. These seek to educate future generations so as to provide an informed and committed constituency for campaigning against genocide and other gross violations of human rights.

An active constituency is certainly crucial in promoting an awareness of contemporary genocide and the need for preventive action, in developing education on human rights in the schools and universities, in gathering information on crisis situations and monitoring them, and above all in campaigning against genocide. International nongovernmental organizations are the obvious core for an effective constituency.

In recent years, there has been a great burgeoning of these nongovernmental human rights organizations seeking to fill the void at the intergovernmental level and more particularly in the United Nations. Their number and diversity testify to the extent of the failure to provide effective protection against violations of human rights. Many of these organizations are, of course, highly specialized, and their effectiveness depends appreciably on close adherence to their specific objectives. Besides, there is a process of imprinting that imparts a passionate devotion to their own causes and does not readily permit extension. But there are many nongovernmental organizations with interests directly or closely related to the prevention of genocide, and several institutes devoted to the study of genocide, such as the pioneer Institute on the Holocaust and Genocide in Israel, the Institute for the Study of Genocide in New York, and the Montreal Institute for Genocide Studies at Concordia University, have now been established.

International Alert against Genocide and Mass Killing is the first nongovernmental organization specifically devoted to campaigning for the prevention of genocide. Our hope is to establish many autonomous units in different parts of the world, which could then be effective at an international level. I have in mind the role of Bahá'í communities in alerting their governments to the threatened genocide against the Bahá'ís in Iran and securing their sympathetic interest. Branches of International Alert established in many different countries could perform a similar function.

Many other organizations are involved in specific campaigns against genocide, such as the International Commission of Jurists, the International League for Human Rights, and the Minority Rights Group. Representatives of indigenous organizations are inevitably forced by the contemporary and historic predatory destruction of indigenous groups to be concerned with the prevention of genocide. There is no dearth of related interests. The problem is that of their coordination for effective campaigning.

Ethnic associations, particularly those representing groups with a history as victims of genocide or other mass killings, should be supportive in campaigns against genocide. But often they are intensely absorbed in their own past trauma and probably need to come to terms with it before they can reach out to other groups. Suffering may in fact be alienating, as in the case of many Jewish groups that would normally be most active supporters of just causes.

There are many reasons for this. Jews tend to view the Holocaust as the culmination of many centuries of anti-Semitism—a view I share. And they are still under threat, with a vast outpouring of anti-Semitism, structured appreciably in the United Nations. Moreover, there are revisionist movements to contend with. In the extreme form of denial of the Holocaust, they lack all credibility. But a more serious movement in Germany sets the Holocaust in the context of the frequent occurrence of genocide, thereby seeking to normalize the Holocaust and deprive it of its specific resonance as a genocide perpetrated with extreme cruelty and much bureaucratic and scientific precision throughout a whole continent against a defenseless and traditionally vilified people. It is to be hoped that Jewish groups can transcend these barriers to participation in a general campaign for the prevention of genocide. Effective campaigning against genocide in general could conceivably make some modest contribution to restraint on annihilatory anti-Semitism: besides, it is consistent with traditional Jewish values.

Religious groups should be active allies in the campaigns against genocide. In the past, they have often been the perpetrators or victims of genocide. And the persecution of religious groups is very much a contemporary phenomenon. A U.N. study of the current dimensions of the problem of intolerance and discrimination on grounds of religion or belief cites innumerable cases of religious persecution.[10]

Complaints of religious discrimination to the United Nations (some of which have elicited action) include the following: the persecution of the Bahá'ís in Iran; the situation in the Socialist People's Republic of Albania, whose constitution explicitly forbade the exercise of the right to freedom of conscience and religion; the promulgation of an ordinance in Pakistan that prima facie violated the right to freedom of thought, expression, conscience, and religion; and the increasing evidence of a policy of religious intolerance in areas under the control of government forces in Afghanistan.

In addition, the report refers to a constant flow of communications in recent years from nongovernmental organizations in which Ahmadis, Bahá'ís, Baptists, Buddhists, Copts, devotees of Hare Krishna, Jehovah's Witnesses, Jews, Lutherans, Muslims, Pentacostalists, Roman Catholics, and Seventh Day Adventists are said to have been imprisoned, tortured, or executed because of the peaceful exercise of their right to freedom of religion.[11]

The geographic spread of these alleged violations is almost worldwide. There are complaints of violations in the Americas and in European, Asian, and African countries. Five Eastern European countries are referred to, a reminder that religious groups are expungible items in the Marxist dialectic.

A further consideration that might be persuasive is that the perpetrators of genocide and their victims are often of different reli-

10. Report by Special Rapporteur, Elizabeth Odio Benito, United Nations E/CN.4/ Sub.2/ 1987/26, dated August 31, 1986.

11. Ibid., para. 59.

gions, even when religious differences are not an issue and there are no obvious manifestations of religious fanaticism or antagonism. This suggests that religious conditioning contributes at a deeper level to a general alienation from victims, facilitating involvement in mass killings. Of course, religious groups are often prominent in denouncing gross violations of human rights through the press and other media and by submissions to intergovernmental organizations. But one would hope for coordinated active involvement in campaigning against the ultimate crime of genocide, which is so intimately related to religious groups.

REFLECTIONS ON EXPERIENCE IN CAMPAIGNING AGAINST GENOCIDE

THE CAMPAIGN IN UGANDA We must assume that moral appeals, not backed by significant pressures or sanctions or inducements, will be ineffective. And here I would like to draw on the experience of International Alert.

When we established International Alert in Los Angeles in March 1985 and in London a month later, our first call for action was against the mass killings in Uganda under the Obote regime. These were certainly more massive and catastrophic than the annihilations under the preceding Amin regime. We followed this up by the formation of a Uganda Watch Committee in London, which campaigned for six months, relating to Ugandan groups and making representations to the British foreign minister responsible for Uganda policy and to the Ugandan High Commissioner. At the same time we sought media publicity as a means for alerting public opinion. Among the members of our committee was Hugh Dinwiddy, dearly beloved by Ugandans, and he prepared regular research reports on the situation in Uganda.

In my own contacts with Ugandans, I was often startled by their innocent faith in the British government. If only the government knew that grandmothers were being killed, and babies, even babies? But I had a very different impression—namely, that the British government was remarkably well informed but feared that Milton Obote, if frustrated by criticism and diplomatic pressure, might turn to the Soviets, with possible domino consequences for British interests in Kenya. As for the Ugandan high commissioner, he fell back on the traditional self-righteous defense of tyrannical governments against charges of atrocity and mass murder: that the opposition Ugandan Resistance Army was composed of bandits, and the government was simply discharging its duty to maintain law and order. (Incidentally, jailers often referred to the unfortunate members of the African National Congress incarcerated in their South African prisons as *bandiet.*)

I then had the inspiration that President Julius Nyerere of Tanzania might be prevailed upon to speak out against the atrocities in Uganda. He had been one of the few African leaders to denounce Amin, and Obote was very much the protégé he had helped install as the new leader following the overthrow of Amin by the Tanzanian army. It seemed to me that he had a duty to denounce the mass murders and other atrocities of the Obote regime and to exercise some restraining influence.

Accordingly, I approached a well-known journalist, formerly the stormy petrel to the administration in the days of British suzerainty; he was said to have good relations with Nyerere. He received me warmly, wrote a strong editorial in a leading journal urging Nyerere to intervene, and gave me an introduction to an official in the Tanzanian High Commissioner's Office, the proper channel, he said, for an approach to Nyerere. When I arrived at the appointed time at the London headquarters of the Tanzanian socialist government, I was startled to find myself in what seemed to be a very conventional bourgeois establishment of black-suited civil servants with all the lineaments of gratified desire. The official with whom I had the appointment was not to be found, and I assumed that he was enjoying his lunch. When he finally arrived, a half hour late, it was clear that he was not indifferent to the fleshpots of London. He heard me out attentively, though perhaps merely ruminating on his lunch, and then declared flatly and blandly that there were no killings in Uganda; it was all newspaper invention. Some two weeks later, when the Ugandan Resistance Army had overthrown Obote, the new government released an estimate of the number of deaths under the Obote regime as about 500,000.

It was, of course, naive of me to suppose that "if only the King knew," in this case the king-maker Nyerere, there would be a positive intervention. Governments respond in terms of their national interests. Even the Galahads in the human rights field, the governments of the Netherlands and Norway, cannot ignore the pressure of their national interests. I am not, however, suggesting that moral values should be ignored. On the contrary, they should be affirmed and reaffirmed, but not relied on as a significant factor in campaigning against genocide and mass killing. In the case of Uganda, effective action was taken by Yoweri Maseveni and his Ugandan Resistance Army, who are now increasingly restoring peaceful normality.

In September 1987, International Alert and Makerere University sponsored a joint conference in Uganda, with the participation of many Ugandan scholars and politicians and visiting international scholars. The conference had the support of the president, and its recommendations were presented to him. These emphasized the need for a political solution to promote national intergration, with acceptance, however, of cultural diversity. Political reconstruction should aim at establishing a grass-roots democracy at all levels of central and community activity, with strong representation of minorities at the center of government. As for the economic institutions, it was recommended that they should be designed to develop a national integrated economy, redressing regional and other imbalances.

These recommendations, of course will be significant only if they are implemented. There has been a follow-up conference, and it is to be hoped that International Alert will be able to assist in securing funds for economic development. But the responsibility and the opportunity to promote ethnic conciliation rest with the government. And for the first time in a generation, the Ugandan government seems equal to the task of restoring peace and harmony.

THE CAMPAIGN IN SRI LANKA In the case of Sri Lanka, there were clear indications of an escalating violent crisis, flowing in part from the consequences of colonial policy but mostly from the strategies pursued by the Sinhalese majority after independence to consolidate its domination over the Tamil minority. Already in 1982, during the initial stages of the founding of International Alert, we had viewed the Sri Lankan conflict as a potential genocidal threat against the Tamils. Action was initiated by an International Emergency Committee in Sri Lanka, which merged with International Alert in 1985. All the indications for effective action were auspicious. The Emergency Committee was a consortium of human rights organizations, including the Netherlands Institute of Human Rights and the Peace Research Institute to Oslo. It was closely associated with aid agencies, and it enjoyed some government support and influential political and human rights leadership.

Sri Lanka at the time was the recipient of a high level of development aid from governments, which it deflected in part to armaments designed for the internal conflict, while its aid strategies served to promote Sinhalese interests and Sinhalese settlement in areas of Tamil predominance. The high level of development aid enjoyed by Sri Lanka provided the means for exerting pressure on the government to resolve the conflict peacefully and this was the strategy International Alert pursued. It informed the Sri Lankan president and cabinet that it would advocate the cessation of aid pending a political settlement acceptable to the peoples of Sri Lanka. But the approach was not purely punitive. International Alert proposed to recommend at the same time the establishment of a fund to assist in the implementation of a peaceful political solution and the rehabilitation of the economy and the well-being of the Sri Lankan people.

The policy of representation to the Sri Lankan government through the World Bank and the aid agencies seemed promising, but it was overtaken and frustrated by deterioration in the internal relations of the contending parties. These internal ethnic conflicts often reach a point when they move under their own, seemingly irreversible, dynamic. The process is familiar. A minority seeks, by endless petitions and pleadings, amelioration of the discrimination under which it suffers. But these are ignored, or derisory reforms are promised, or substantial reforms which are not implemented, driving the minority leaders to more radical demands. At this stage the government may respond by punitive action against the leaders, proscribing their organizations, and suspending the enjoyment of many conventional human rights by imposing states of emergency. There may be a resort to violence by the government or by members of the majority group with some government complicity. Then, by a process that René Lemarchand describes as *l'engrenage de la violence,* the conflict moves out of control to indiscriminate reciprocal violence, with the government finally deciding to deploy its overwhelming power in a military solution, with an inevitably large toll of civilian deaths.

This is more or less what happened in Sri Lanka, precipitating intervention by the Indian army. The conciliatory policies advocated by International Alert and backed by economic pressures foundered as a result of the polarizing effects of reciprocal indiscriminate terrorism, religious legitimation by Sinhalese Buddhist monks of mass murder and atrocity, the unleashing of the army on a civilian population in a campaign to suppress the rebel forces, and the self-interested involvement of great powers. Now, however, with the appointment of a new president, the establishment of provincial councils, and some movement toward conciliation, International Alert has renewed its activities.

THE CAMPAIGN IN BURUNDI The recent massacres in Burundi are a particular reproach. They appear to have been a reenactment on a smaller scale of the army massacres in 1972, though arising from different precipitating events and in a less oppressive political context; and they were anticipated as embedded in the situation and predictable because of the consolidation of Tutsi-Hima domination and exclusive control of power. And yet nothing was done; and one recalls the support by the Organization of African Unity (OAU) for the regime in the first massacres and generally the hesitation of the

OAU to intervene in internal conflicts. But it is difficult to know what could have been done.

Prior to independence, the relations between the Tutsi minority of some 14 percent and the Hutu majority of 85 percent were fluid, with many relations across ethnic lines, much intermarriage, and territorial intermingling. And there was a political party committed to national integration under the leadership of a popular prince. All the indications for ethnic harmony were favorable, and there was little reason to predict ethnic polarization. But in the neighboring territory of Rwanda, struggles for power between the ruling Tutsi and the majority Hutu had ended in Hutu domination and large-scale massacres of Tutsi. These were traumatic and threatening events for the Tutsi minority in Burundi, while encouraging Hutu leaders to hope for Hutu domination in Burundi.

The result was that following independence and the overthrow of the king, Burundi society rapidly polarized, with political division flowing along ethnic lines. And after a series of violent confrontations, the Tutsi army engaged in reprisal massacres, taking the form of a preemptive strike against the emergence of a Hutu leadership. Murdering bands even reached down into the schools for their Hutu victims in an operation René Lemarchand describes as selective genocide.[12] The Hutu death toll in 1982 numbered about 100,000, and there were further massacres in later years. The Tutsi response, far from being conciliatory, was to institutionalize its superiority, with most of the key institutions, including the army, almost totally Tutsi.

The new regime, which assumed power in 1987, is more responsive to the need for reform, but given the background of past conflict and current fears, it was not surprising that rural confrontation should precipitate a massacre of Tutsi by Hutu and massive reprisal massacres by the Tutsi army.

The present regime, in contrast to its predecessor's response to the 1982 genocide, is committed to reconciliation. The president has

12. René Lemarchand, *Selective Genocide in Burundi* (London: Minority Rights Group, 1974).

appointed a national commission to study the problem of ethnic violence in Burundi. He has reconstituted the cabinet to provide equal representation for Hutu and appointed a Hutu prime minister, and there have been high-level discussions between representatives of Rwanda and Burundi.

There seems now to be a basis for a human rights movement with participation by government representatives of Uganda, Rwanda, Burundi, and Tanzania. The Organization of African Unity suffers from many of the defects of the United Nations, and the best prospect for an effective African human rights movement lies in regional associations.

INTERNATIONAL ALERTS

Two international alerts were issued by the international secretariat, dealing with the serious ethnic conflicts in Suriname and Fiji. The Los Angeles division organized international conferences on Sri Lanka and the Punjab. In the case of Sri Lanka, in addition to an information function, there was hope that the Tamils and Sinhalese attending might agree on measures for conciliation, which could perhaps help defuse the conflict. In the result, the conference was more remarkable for unleashing the passions that stand in the way of ethnic conciliation. Promising postconference discussions designed to arrive at a mutually agreed policy were proceeding well, but they were finally frustrated by the intervention of a high Catholic dignitary who immediately invited the participation of a Sinhalese extremist. The Punjab conference developed essentially as a Sikh conference, with little participation by Hindus, but it effectively conveyed the oppressive mishandling of the Sikh campaign for self-determination. Representations made to the U.S. and Indian governments recommending policies to be pursued in relation to Sri Lanka and the Punjab were without effect.

And finally, mention should be made of a conference under the joint auspices of International Alert and the Netherlands Institute of Human Rights, which analyzed the resurgence of racism in Europe and the need for preventive action. Copies of the report on the conference under the title *New Expressions of Racism in Europe* are available from the Netherlands Institute.

POTENTIALITIES FOR PREVENTIVE ACTION

Given the restraints on the restructuring of offending societies and the limited and supplicant access to centers of power, what realistic contributions can nongovernmental organizations be expected to make for the prevention of genocide?

A primary long-term task is the building of a constituency for active campaigning against the threat of genocide. It should be associated with an educational program to promote an informed awareness of genocide and a commitment to preventive action, as discussed above. The objective is the promotion of a social movement comparable to the peace movement, but with the realization that the motivation for participation would be predominantly altruistic, in contrast to the peace movement, which draws on the omnipresent fear of annihilation in an age of nuclear armaments.

With a wide geographical spread of participating organizations, the opportunities for effective action against threatened genocides are greatly extended. There is the possibility of enlisting the support of a number of governments as a basis for effective lobbying in intergovernmental organizations, along the lines of the Bahá'í campaign against annihilatory persecution in Iran. Then, too, there are likely to be creative opportunities for local initiatives, adding to the potential momentum of the campaign. And, finally, International Alerts have greater resonance with wide supporting interest. Failing this, even excellently prepared statements are evanescent, seemingly destined for immediate oblivion.

In planning strategies for the formidable task of campaigning against genocide, there is a need to guard against the conception of genocide as a unified phenomenon. At a high level of abstraction—as, for example, the international legal definition—it constitutes a distinctive crime. In reality, the manifestations of genocide are quite diverse, with distinctive processes affecting varied groups in different social settings. I have tended to view this diversity from the perspective of the victimized groups, differentiating, on the one hand, between groups perpetually at risk (the hunting and gathering groups and the hostage groups, such as European Jews or middleman minorities) and, on the other hand, the more general case, particularly in the third world, of ethnic, racial, religious, and national groups becoming victims of genocide or mass killings in struggles for power, or for freedom from discrimination, or a measure of autonomy, or indeed separation.

The varied processes associated with this diversity of annihilatory contexts offer different possibilities for preventive action. The destruction of hunting and gathering groups tends to be the least accessible to monitoring and preventive action. They maintain few, if any, relations with other groups, and their annihilation has little significance for the wider society. Their habitats are usually remote areas, removed from contact and visibility, and their victimizers are generally invading groups of settlers or development agencies. When governments intervene on behalf of the victims, their intervention tends to be half-hearted or inept, offering little protection against the undermining of the culture and the ultimate destruction of the group. The outside world generally reacts with indifference to the fate of these groups, save where there are broader and more threatening implications, as in the ecological destruction consequent upon the deforestation in the Amazon basin.

The destruction of hostage groups is sometimes predictable, preceded by mounting campaigns of vilification and a crescendo of hostile encounters, as, for example, in Uganda prior to the expulsion of Indians by Amin. At other times, the hostile action against hostage groups is suddenly precipitated by internal or external conflicts not directly related to the groups. The expulsion of these groups and the murderous attacks on them have many repercussions in the host society, and they may be well received in the outside world, save for exasperation at the pressure to confer refugee status. The circumstances often do not favor preventive action.

The prospects for preventive action in the struggles for the restructuring of group relations are more promising, at any rate, in the early stages of the conflict. There are many case studies of polarization of relations between racial, ethnic, religious, and national groups in plural societies, and the processes are well enough known. They often extend over an appreciable period of time and are characterized by many gross violations of human rights, which provide occasion for alerting international opinion to the destructive potentialities of the conflict. The means available for intervention are a variety of pressures, as, for example, ventilating the issues in international forums, withholding aid, or offering such inducements as assistance in development to attain a more equitable regional balance, if this is one of the issues in the conflict. The approach needs to be conciliatory, seeking to enlist the cooperation of both parties to the conflict and avoiding confrontation, save in dealings with intransigent regimes.

The many conflicts in the contemporary world that carry the threat of annihilatory violence give rise to a dilemma of choice. In practice, the selection of cases probably tends to be somewhat haphazard. Development agencies may be concerned that, as a result of internal conflicts, the aid they provide is being deflected from its intended purpose. Or there may be an abiding interest in a country with many personal contacts and associations and a desire to assist in promoting conciliation in a threatening internal conflict. Or some catastrophe may attract international attention and call for an International Alert. All these are appropriate motivations, but they can easily lead to an erratic selection of cases. Moreover, with so many destructive conflicts demanding immediate intervention, there may be a tendency to overextend one's resources, leading to a superficiality of approach in situations that call for careful planning and continuity in the slow processes of conciliation and reconstruction. Clearly, we need to establish criteria for the selection of cases.

I would suggest the following criteria—first, the assumption of a supporting role where there are already nongovernmental organizations working for the protection of particular groups. Thus, Cultural

Survival and Survival International are essentially concerned with the prevention of genocide against indigenous groups, including hunters and gatherers, and this is, of course, also a major concern of a variety of organized indigenous groups. One hopes it would be possible to support their campaigns against the threat of genocide.

This would permit, as a second criterion, concentration on the protection of other groups. The London division of International Alert concentrates on ethnic conciliation in situations of threatening destructive conflict. This might be broadened to a focus on violent conflict affecting the interrelations of racial, ethnic, religious, and national sections of plural societies. Their struggles for the restructuring of group interrelations are frequently associated with gross violations of human rights, including mass killings and genocide. They are, in fact, a major source of genocidal conflicts, particularly, but not exclusively, in the third world.

The final criterion should be the possibility of making a contribution toward the prevention of genocide. Clearly, in the early stages of campaigning the approach must necessarily be exploratory, as experience is gained on campaigning in different social contexts.

For many years, the structure of international relations was by no means favorable for preventive action against genocide. The cold war between the superpowers was a major contributor to genocidal conflict in many parts of the world. Amelioration of their relations could greatly enhance the opportunities for effective campaigning against genocide. And the present change in Soviet policy, and a cooperative response by the United States, may be a significant step in that direction.

A further development with potentiality for the prevention of genocide is the ratification by the United States of the Genocide Convention. Since the United Nations has failed to take significant action for either the prevention or the punishment of the crime of genocide, notwithstanding ratification of the convention by almost a hundred states, it is clear that ratification itself has little intrinsic significance. But it does provide an opportunity to activate the United States to use its aid policies, trade relations, and diplomatic and other resources to resume the leading role in the prevention of genocide that it took in the Nuremberg trials and in the framing of the Genocide Convention.

Ervin Staub   *Chapter 10*

TRANSFORMING THE BYSTANDERS: ALTRUISM, CARING, AND SOCIAL RESPONSIBILITY

AUTHOR'S NOTE: The roots of my lifelong concern with helping and harm-doing obviously are my experiences as a young Jewish child in Hungary facing the evils of the Holocaust, while also experiencing the wonderful caring and courage demonstrated by a Christian woman who worked for my family in helping us and other Jews. I survived in a "protected house" as a result of the heroic actions of Raoul Wallenberg. When I started my first job at Harvard I began research on sharing and helping behavior. But for years I looked at my work as guided simply by "scientific" interest, and only gradually did I fully acknowledge its personal sources.

Currently I am a professor of psychology at the University of Massachusetts at Amherst. In addition to articles, I have published several books on my research and theory about the personal and social determinants of helping and altruism and their development in children and on passivity in the face of others' need. In the last decade I have also been writing about the origins of human destructiveness. My book, *The Roots of Evil: The Origins of*

Genocide and Other Group Violence (Cambridge: Cambridge University Press, 1989) is about the cultural and psychological roots of many kinds of group violence; it also explores the evolution of caring and nonaggressive persons and societies.

What are the roots of caring, helping, altruism, and socially responsible action? We have substantial research on what leads people to respond to others' needs[1] and, conversely, on what inhibits people from helping others—why they remain passive bystanders when they witness the mistreatment and suffering of an individual or a group.[2] The research can help us understand and develop theories about the influences that lead people to take action to prevent their society from harming subgroups within it or to stop the escalating mistreatment of subgroups. What might lead them to protest the mistreatment of people in other nations and to attempt to influence their government to act in behalf of such people? What might lead them to try to protect their own group from self-destructive actions like environmental pollution or the escalation of hostility toward other nations that may end in war? In brief, how can people be mobilized to engage in socially responsible actions?

In this chapter I will examine the personal characteristics of individuals that can, in combination with certain circumstances, lead to altruism, or the unselfish helping of others. I will trace the psychological processes that lead to altruistic behavior—even to the point sometimes of an individual placing himself in extreme danger in order to help another. I will then present the findings of research on the childhood origins of altruistic behavior—the child-rearing practices that give rise to a caring adult. Finally, I will examine at length the bystander phenomenon: why people remain passive in the face

1. N. Eisenberg, *Altruistic Emotion, Cognition and Behavior* (Hillsdale, N.J.: Lawrence Erlbaum Associates, 1986); Ervin Staub, *Positive Social Behavior and Morality,* vol. 1, *Social and Personal Influences* (New York: Academic Press, 1978); Ervin Staub, *Positive Social Behavior and Morality,* vol. 2, *Socialization and Development* (New York: Academic Press, 1979).

2. Ervin Staub, *The Roots of Evil: The Origins of Genocide and Other Group Violence* (Cambridge: Cambridge University Press, 1989).

of other people's suffering or of societal needs and what we can do to change their behavior.

PERSONAL CHARACTERISTICS AND PSYCHOLOGICAL PROCESSES

Three types of motives have been identified as sources of altruism. The first, a *prosocial value orientation,* is an important personal characteristic that can lead to altruism. As measured in research, a prosocial orientation is characterized by a positive evaluation of human beings and a feeling of personal responsibility for others' welfare. The focus is on others' welfare; the motivation is to improve others' welfare. Several studies have shown that individuals with a strong prosocial value orientation are more helpful than others.[3] A second major class of motivation is *moral-rule orientation.* Here the individual acts according to moral rules that prescribe help for other people. A third type of motivation is *empathy,* or the form of it usually called sympathy. All three can be either psychological processes—thoughts and feelings—within individuals that give rise to and guide action or personal characteristics, the dispositions for these psychological processes. It is likely that empathy and prosocial value orientation share certain components, that characteristics like the positive evaluation of others and caring about their welfare enter into both.

In the *theory of personal goals* that I have presented elsewhere I suggest that we need to consider, first, the motives of individuals that lead them to help.[4] But because people have many, potentially

3. J. K. Feinberg, "Anatomy of a Helping Situation: Some Personality and Situational Determinants of Helping in a Conflict Situation Involving Another's Psychological Distress" (Ph.D. diss., University of Massachusetts, Amherst, 1978); S. M. Grodman, "The Role of Personality and Situational Variables in Responding to and Helping an Individual in Psychological Distress" (Ph.D. diss., University of Massachusetts, Amherst, 1979); Ervin Staub, "Helping a Distressed Person: Social, Personality and Stimulus Determinants," in *Advances in Experimental Social Psychology,* vol. 7, ed. L. Berkowitz (New York: Academic Press, 1974); Staub, *Positive Social Behavior,* vol. 1.

4. Staub, *Positive Social Behavior,* vol. 1; Ervin Staub, ed., "Social and Prosocial

conflicting motives, we need to consider the hierarchy of their values and goals and the position within that hierarchy of those values and goals that motivate altruism and helping. Second, we need to consider supporting characteristics, such as competencies or role taking, that determine what motives are expressed in action and when they become active. To understand and predict specific actions we need to consider the activating potential of the environment for various goals and potential goal conflicts and their resolution.

To understand altruism we also must consider the individual's moral inclusiveness or exclusiveness. I have suggested that values and goals have ranges of applicability that can differ greatly among people, defining the circumstances or the individuals to which they apply.[5] For example, an important characteristic of rescuers of Jews in Nazi Europe was their sense of inclusiveness—the extent to which they included people from groups other than their own as part of humanity to whom moral considerations apply.[6] A variety of psychological processes (devaluation, just-world thinking, and so on) can lead to moral exclusion, with great variation among individuals and groups in their use.[7]

Motivations are rarely pure. People can have integrated personal goals, in which potentially conflicting goals and values join and a single course of action leads to the satisfaction of all of them. At times self-oriented and other-oriented motives combine: a person for whom competence and success are important may satisfy these motives through the successful fulfillment of moral and altruistic values.

Behavior: Personal and Situational Influences and Their Interactions," in *Personality: Basic Aspects and Current Research* (Englewood Cliffs, N.J.: Prentice-Hall, 1980); Ervin Staub, "A Conception of the Determinants and Development of Altruism and Aggression: Motives, the Self, the Environment," in *Altruism and Aggression: Social and Biological Origins,* ed. C. Zahn-Waxler et al. (Cambridge: Cambridge University Press, 1986); Staub, *The Roots of Evil.*

5. Staub, *Positive Social Behavior,* vol. 1; Staub, "Social and Prosocial Behavior."

6. S. B. Oliner and P. Oliner, *The Altruistic Personality: Rescuers of Jews in Nazi Europe* (New York: Free Press, 1988).

7. Staub, *The Roots of Evil;* Ervin Staub, "Moral Exclusion, Personal Goal Theory and Extreme Destructiveness," *Journal of Social Issues* (special issue, "The Scope of Justice," ed. S. Opawa) 46 (1990): 47–65.

Alternatively, ideological and self-oriented motives can combine in perpetrators of harm: a torturer may work hard to be better than others in extracting information from prisoners.[8]

The value of caring (which appears to be similar to prosocial orientation), or moral principles such a justice, and of empathy have all been identified as important motivators of heroic rescues. In a recent study normocentrism—membership in and connection to a group and its norms—was found to be another important motivation.[9] This motivation can be widespread, as it was in Belgium where the majority of the population resisted the persecution of Jews.[10] There is a problematic aspect of such motivation, however. As Nechama Tec reported, some Polish priests encouraged people to help Jews, but others encouraged them to help the Nazis in the identification and expulsion of Jews, which were steps leading to their extermination.[11] A connection to the group and normocentric motivation can lead people to help or harm others, depending on the direction the group and its leaders take.

CHILDHOOD ORIGINS

Research findings and theory based on them suggest that parents' ways of relating to their children and certain child-rearing practices are important sources of an altruistic disposition.[12] These include treating children affectionately and reasoning with them—explaining rules and especially pointing out to them the consequences of their behavior on others. Also valuable is firm discipline; parents

8. Frantz Fanon, *The Wretched of the Earth* (1961; New York: Grove Press, 1968); Ervin Staub, "The Psychology and Culture of Torture and Torturers," in *Psychology and Torture*, ed. P. Suedfeld (New York: Hemisphere Publishing Group, 1990).

9. Oliner and Oliner, *The Altruistic Personality.*

10. Helen Fein, *Accounting for Genocide: National Responses and Jewish Victimization during the Holocaust* (New York: Free Press, 1979).

11. Nechama Tec, *When Light Pierced the Darkness: Christian Rescue of Jews in Nazi-occupied Poland* (New York: Oxford University Press, 1986).

12. Eisenberg, *Altruistic Emotion, Cognition and Behavior;* Staub, *Positive Social Behavior,* vol. 2; Staub, "A Conception of the Determinants."

should insist that the child behave according to important values and standards, but with limited assertion of the parents' own power and little or no physical punishment. Children must experience caring if they are to see people in a positive light so that they value them rather than fear or hate them. And they must be made aware of others' feelings and needs. The parents' example is also important, of course—how helpful and socially responsible they are outside the family.

Children should be guided to help others so that they can learn from the experience. My own and others' research shows that both children and adults learn by doing.[13] Given supportive conditions, once people begin to help others, they become increasingly helpful, with changes in their views of others and themselves. People also learn violence by doing; as they harm others, they become increasingly capable of harmful action.[14]

Frequently, intense persistent helping is an outcome of such an evolution. Those helping others come to value the beneficiaries of their actions more, become more committed to their welfare, and come to see themselves as more helpful individuals and thus willing to make even greater sacrifices. And an intense commitment to a particular individual or group can evolve into a commitment to human welfare in general.

Such an evolution took place, for example, in the case of Oscar Schindler, a Nazi factory owner in Poland who first simply responded to his Jewish slave laborers as human beings and ended up saving twelve hundred lives.[15] It also characterized the Mothers of the Plaza del Mayo in Argentina, who gathered to protest the disappearance of their own children, then developed a concern about all the "disappeared," and finally became committed to human welfare in general. To some extent this progression characterized Raoul Wallenberg and other rescuers.[16]

13. Staub, *Positive Social Behavior,* vol. 2.
14. Staub, *The Roots of Evil.*
15. T. Keneally, *Schindler's List* (New York: Penguin, 1983).
16. Staub, *The Roots of Evil.*

In apparent contrast to an evolving or escalating sense of altruism is "spontaneous helping." In the face of an urgent need some people respond at once, without the decision-making process that normally precedes helping. This happens in emergencies that require immediate action.[17] Many rescuers in one study reported that when asked to help they decided to do so without hesitation. Other reports have indicated that people who engage in extreme helpfulness—for example, donating bone marrow—remember having made an instant decision with no question in their minds that they would help. The decision-making process is likely to be short-circuited in people who possess motives for helping and feel competent to help when they face others' intense need. For some helpers, however, especially rescuers, the memory of the initial decision making may be overshadowed by their history of rescue, by the intense sense of commitment they have developed,[18] and perhaps by the fact that helping has become a way of life.

THE PASSIVITY OF BYSTANDERS

People often remain passive both in the face of the mistreatment of groups of people, such as discrimination, torture, mass killing, and genocide, and in the face of events in their society that harm or endanger everyone, such as the destruction of the environment or the nuclear arms race. Socially responsible action is both similar to and different from helping and altruism directed at individuals. To the extent it derives from a feeling of responsibility, its focus is the social good, which includes one's own good but extends to one's group, other groups, and possibly all of humanity. Some of our knowledge of bystander passivity comes from researchers on emergency helping[19]

17. Staub, *Positive Social Behavior,* vol. 1.
18. Oliner and Oliner, *The Altruistic Personality.*
19. B. Latane and J. Darley, *The Unresponsive Bystander: Why Doesn't He Help?* (New York: Appleton-Century-Crofts, 1970); Staub, *Positive Social Behavior,* vol. 1.

and some from analyses of the psychology of perpetrators, by-standers, and heroic helpers in genocides and mass killings.[20]

TYPE I BYSTANDERS: PASSIVITY IN THE FACE OF INDIVIDUAL'S MIS-TREATMENT There are two categories of Type I bystanders. Those who witness the mistreatment of members of a group of their own society but remain passive are internal bystanders. They may accept demands by the perpetrators that they participate in the persecution, even gradually joining the group. Their silence and their semiactive role often encourage the perpetrators. For example, in Nazi Germany most Germans participated to a greater or lesser degree in the system the Nazis established. They boycotted stores, owned by Jews, broke off relations with Jewish friends, and so on. Some even initiated anti-Jewish actions before the government ordered them to—businesses fired Jewish employees or refused to give them paid vacations.[21] Other nations and outside groups who remain passive are external bystanders. By maintaining friendly relations with an offending nation, they also encourage the perpetrators. Coming to understand the psychology of bystanders, internal and external, can help us arrive at ways to increase caring and social responsibility.

Internal bystanders may legitimately fear an often brutal system, but that is an insufficient explanation for their passivity. In Germany people protested against the euthanasia program and brought it (though not all the killings) to an end,[22] but they did not protest the persecution of Jews. Outsiders may remain silent even when they have nothing to fear—as did the nations of the world and the corporations that conducted business with Germany between 1933 and 1939. Like internal bystanders, they come to support the persecutors through important symbolic gestures. The Olympics were held in

20. Staub, *The Roots of Evil*.
21. R. Hilberg, *The Destruction of the European Jews* (New York: Harper and Row, 1961).
22. Robert J. Lifton, *The Nazi Doctors: Medical Killing and the Psychology of Genocide* (New York: Basic Books, 1986).

Germany in 1936, for example, and Jewish runners were withdrawn from a U.S. relay team though Germany did not request it. And the United States sold oil to Germany in the mid-thirties, which helped its air war against Republican Spain.

Internal Bystanders. Internal bystanders remain passive partly because they share a cultural-societal tilt with the perpetrators. The groundwork is laid for mass killings or genocide in a society when it experiences extremely difficult conditions, like economic problems, intense political conflict, and the social disorganization that arises from them. These combine with certain cultural characteristics or preconditions for group violence, including a history of devaluation of a subgroup within the society; an overly strong respect for authority; a monolithic quality arising from a limited number of dominant values and little freedom for individuals to express contrary beliefs and values; a group self-concept of superiority, or strong vulnerability, or their combination; and a history of aggressive conflict resolution.

The material deprivation resulting from economic problems is usually difficult to satisfy, so that people's attention turns to fulfilling psychological needs arising from the combination of difficult life conditions and cultural characteristics: they seek to protect and elevate the self, to comprehend a chaotic and changing reality, to establish connections with and support from other people, to regain hope. As a result of the cultural characteristics listed above, which create a predisposition for group violence, the methods people use to satisfy these needs may turn them against a subgroup of the society. They may elevate the self over others through devaluation and violence, engage in scapegoating, adopt a nationalistic or "better-world" ideology that offers a vision of the future, comprehension, and hope; they may join groups that are working to fulfill the "higher ideals" of the ideology. The bystanders share with perpetrators the cultural background, the experience of difficult conditions, the needs these give rise to, and possibly even an inclination for the methods perpetrators use to fulfill these needs.[23]

The devaluation of victims, which usually has long-standing cultural roots, preselects them as scapegoats and ideological enemies. Once the perpetrator group begins to harm the victims, learning by participation, with its resulting change in perpetrators and the society, makes progressively increasing harm-doing possible. Individuals and the group change step by step along a continuum of destruction. The shared cultural tilt together with the self-focus created by difficult conditions contribute to the passivity of bystanders.

But passivity in the face of others' suffering changes people. Bystanders evolve just as perpetrators of harm do . As they observe the victims' suffering, just-world thinking—the tendency to believe that the world is just, so people who suffer must deserve their fate owing to their actions or character—leads bystanders to further devalue the victims.[24] They decrease their involvement, their empathic distress, their feelings of responsibility, by distancing themselves from the victims. They assume an objectifying perceptual stance that diminishes empathy. They may join the perpetrators in "moral equilibration"—the replacement of moral standards that prohibit harming people with others that justify or permit the victims' mistreatment, such as respect for authority or loyalty to leaders. Over time, they exclude the victims from the moral universe and change their views of themselves. They become willing to accept the victims' suffering, for what they come to regard as good reasons.[25]

In sum, contributing to the passivity of bystanders are their societal tilt, their own strong needs, the difficulty of separating themselves from the group and especially of speaking out against its harmful actions, a moral exclusion that results from devaluation, the process of scapegoating, the perceived higher ideals of an ideology, and their

23. Staub, *The Roots of Evil.*
24. M. Lerner, *The Belief in a Just World: A Fundamental Delusion* (New York: Plenum, 1980).
25. Staub, *The Roots of Evil.*

evolution as they passively witness others' suffering and their society moves along a continuum of destruction. The more bystanders are tied to their group, the more difficult it is for them to oppose it. The longer they remain passive, the more they will be resocialized in their beliefs, values, and behavior, which makes action on their part progressively less likely. As they change, some join the perpetrators, as did, for example, some members of the Berlin Psychoanalytic Institute during the Nazi years.[26] The changing norms and institutions of the society, and the evolving commitment of perpetrators to the destruction of their victims—which further decrease their tolerance for opposition—progressively diminish the likelihood that opposition will be effective.

External Bystanders. Just-world thinking and the tendency to devalue those who suffer also characterize external bystanders. In addition, often there has been a long-standing devaluation of certain victim groups, such as Jews or, in the West, Asian people (the victims of the autogenocide in Cambodia) or, in the United States, communists. The propaganda of the perpetrators about the evil nature of victims often affects external bystanders as well. Material self-interest, such as trade with the perpetrators, also enters the picture. All these factors influenced the United States and European countries between 1933 and 1939 and resulted in an increase in anti-Semitism everywhere. As external bystanders remain passive, they too learn by doing, which may lead to diminished concern for the victims—a progressively increasing devaluation of them and moral exclusion.

TYPE II BYSTANDERS: PASSIVITY IN THE FACE OF SOCIETAL ISSUES
One reason for passivity among Type II bystanders is that the goals and values that predominate in a society may be contrary to car-

26. V. Friedrich, "From Psychoanalysis to the 'Great Treatment': Psychoanalysis under National Socialism," *Political Psychology* 10 (1989): 3–26; Ervin Staub, "Steps along the Continuum of Destruction: The Evolution of Bystanders: German Psychoanalysts and Lessons for Today," *Political Psychology* 10 (1989): 39–53.

ing and social responsibility. Acquisitiveness, a focus on self-interest, and an individualism that conflicts with and diminishes feelings of connection and community make moral values and social responsibility less important in the hierarchy of individual and group goals.

Another reason is that people tend to respond to the immediate. Earning a living, caring for children, and fulfilling everyday responsibilities are urgent tasks that detract from the impulse to take action toward fulfilling long-term group goals. The need to perform one's daily tasks is powerful enough to dominate even those people who have strong motives that promote caring and social responsibility. Moreover, it is one thing to have other-oriented goals and values and feel personal responsibility for the welfare of other individuals and another thing to feel responsible for broad human issues like the fate of minorities or the poor, the environment, or nuclear disarmament. Concern for broader issues, in most people, seems less developed, which makes internal activation of social goals and values unlikely. And to the extent that issues are abstract and remote, external activation is also less likely.

Diffusion of responsibility and pluralistic ignorance are other inhibitors of socially responsible feelings and action.[27] Some people may feel that it is the government's responsibility to act; others, that everyone in the group or all of humanity share the responsibility, thus diminishing individual responsibility and absolving the individual from the need to act. When there is limited public discussion of an issue, a condition of pluralistic ignorance exists. If no one seems concerned, the issue seems unimportant and action unnecessary. In addition, the authorities often define opposition to official policies (which may be creating or at least not addressing the problems) as unpatriotic and disloyal.

Finally, given the magnitude of societal problems, the individual's feeling of powerlessness inhibits action. Even if motives are strong, they will not be expressed in action unless the individual has some

27. Latane and Darley, *The Unresponsive Bystander*.

faith in the possibility of their fulfillment. How can one person stop discrimination and persecution of minorities or the devastation of the environment? In the real world, people acting alone have little influence in such large matters.

Given inaction, individuals shift awareness away from these issues to lessen their feelings of danger, personal responsibility, and guilt. The result is often call *denial,* although it does not fit the traditional psychoanalytic meaning of the term. Thoughts about such matters are avoided, but the issues are probably not repressed or denied in the psychoanalytic sense. Another term, *psychic numbing,* has been used to explain the relatively passive acceptance by people of the nuclear arms race in spite of the dangers it poses, but that term, too, does not seem to fit the phenomenon well. Psychic numbing is a diminished emotional responsiveness that results from severe trauma, such as the experience of nuclear attack in Hiroshima or other intense bombing, the experience of survivors of Nazi concentration camps, or the experience of combat.[28] It is unlikely to result from daily life in a Western post-industrial society, however threatening the possibility of nuclear war.

Perhaps similar and more straightforward explanations are the following. First, there is a kind of gating or screening of phenomena, given the overload of events in the modern world impinging on us. This is similar to Stanley Milgram's description of what happens to inhabitants of large cities.[29] Second, there is inattention to and avoidance of events and information that have a negative emotional impact on us, especially if we do not believe we have the capacity to deal with them, to control them. Nonetheless, desensitization and inattention to social issues are not of such a nature that people cannot be mobilized for action.

28. Robert J. Lifton, *The Broken Connection: On Death and the Continuity of Life* (New York: Touchstone Books, 1979).
29. Stanley Milgram, "The Experience of Living in Cities," *Science* 167 (1970): 1461–1468.

MOBILIZING BYSTANDERS

It is useful to know first, what one hopes to accomplish by mobilizing bystanders. Ultimately, I would hope for a world in which human relationships are characterized by caring and connection, in the relations both of individuals and of groups. Human rights would be respected, which means not only safety from physical harm but also fulfillment of basic needs for food and shelter and thus at least minimal social justice. In the world I seek, individuals' psychological needs would not be met at the expense of others, and genuine conflicts would not be resolved through aggression. Connection and caring for others would be valued more than wealth and power. This would require at least a minimal feeling of security, which the group must provide; otherwise security will be sought by means of acquiring wealth and power.[30] A view of shared interests would contribute to socially responsible action.

For such a world to come about, children and adults in the long run must develop certain personal characteristics, such as a prosocial value orientation and empathy. As I noted earlier, socialization in the home and schools and certain experiences with other people shape these characteristics. Members of groups, whether nations or subgroups of societies, must develop an appreciation of one another's humanity. They need to initiate positive acts and respond to others' positive acts, which promotes reciprocity. Systems of positive reciprocity can be expanded by joint enterprises serving shared goals that are superordinate to individual and potentially conflicting goals. The realms for shared goals can include the environment, nuclear arms, economic cooperation, and other such matters. To further evolve and maintain positive connections with and views of others, people need to develop cross-cutting relations; members of different groups must be integrated in their living, working, and playing together.[31]

30. Staub, *The Roots of Evil*.
31. Ibid.

THE VALUE OF SELF-AWARENESS AND INFORMATION Self-awareness can minimize the impact of the psychological processes that inhibit caring, helping, and socially responsible actions and that promote moral exclusion. Disseminating information and education can
be extremely useful to create self-awareness. Building awareness both
of human tendencies for us-them differentiation and for devaluing
those who suffer and of how the words and actions of other bystanders may inhibit us from responding to individual suffering and
societal problems can reduce the power of such inhibitory forces. My
belief in this is fortified by my impression of greater sensitivity in
students exposed to such information and by research showing that
information about inhibiting conditions increases later helping behavior in emergencies.[32]

Education needs to go beyond the simple dissemination of information, however. It should include training and experience that help
people observe and catch themselves devaluing sufferers or thinking
that victims have brought on their suffering by their own actions or
character and thus deserve to suffer. It needs to raise awareness in
people of the influence of their own needs on their thinking and
actions.

Providing information serves another purpose. Frequently people
avoid becoming involved with others' needs, or with societal and
world issues, as they busily pursue their own private lives. But if they
become aware of the intensity and urgency of the needs of other
people or of problems in their society and the world, they are more
likely to take action. The outpouring of aid to starving Ethiopians
in the mid-1980s was stimulated by a television program about them.

Information about the lives, circumstances, feelings, habits, and
customs of people who are persecuted or of those with persistent
need (such as the homeless) can increase individuals' attention and
concern. Education and information that stresses the shared humanity of different groups of people, their shared needs and aspirations,

32. A. Beaman, et al. "Increasing Helping Rates through Information Dissemination: Teaching Pays," *Personality and Social Psychology Bulletin* 4 (1978): 406–411.

can promote their inclusion in one's moral realm. It can also lead to a consideration of the balance of one's own and others' needs and awareness of one's advantage, which can activate caring. Information that expands knowledge about the environment, nuclear arms, the economic interdependence of the world, and problematic government policies will expand cognitive networks and the impact of these issues on thought, feelings, and action.

Abstractions do not suffice to humanize persons and groups, and to bring to life general societal and global issues. As Tversky and Kahneman have suggested, people need "availability heuristics," images or memories by which they can make hypothetical possibilities real.[33] Facts alone do not provide these heuristics. Distant issues must be brought near both by enlarging knowledge about them through the creation of availability heuristics—that is, by making real the suffering of people or the potential impact of conditions like environmental pollution on individual lives—and by showing their relevance for the self and for important personal goals.

To help individuals overcome the feeling of personal helplessness, information should be disseminated about the tremendous potential power of bystanders. There is much evidence showing that people can greatly influence the behavior of others. This has been demonstrated in both experimental research[34] and real-life events.[35] For example, in Nazi Europe the behavior of a sympathetic population[36] and that of a group of helpers-rescuers[37] repeatedly influenced not only other bystanders but also perpetrators. The nineteenth-century abolitionists are another example of the impact strong commitment

33. A. Tversky and D. Kahneman, "Judgment under Uncertainty: Heuristics and Biases," *Science* 185 (1974): 1124–1131.

34. L. Bickman, "Social Influence and Diffusion of Responsibility in an Emergency," *Journal of Experimental and Social Psychology* 8 (1972): 438–445; Staub, "Helping a Distressed Person."

35. Staub, *The Roots of Evil*.

36. Fein, *Accounting for Genocide*.

37. P. P. Hallie, *Lest Innocent Blood Be Shed: The Story of the Village of Le Chambon, and How Goodness Happened There* (New York: Harper and Row, 1979); Staub, *The Roots of Evil*.

can have. Research findings have also shown that a minority, by clearly and strongly expressing its attitudes and beliefs, can greatly influence majority views.[38]

But even when individuals become aware of the potential of bystanders to exert influence, they can still feel personally helpless and ineffective if they do not know avenues for effective action. They need to learn how they, if they act, can contribute to ultimate goals and to become aware of meaningful intermediate goals—in other words, how to measure and appreciate progress. Other factors that encourage continued involvement in efforts that usually bring only slow results include support by like-minded others, strong values, and as a result of engaging in action, the development of a principled commitment to action itself.

In fact, antinuclear activists, in contrast to nonactivists, tend to believe more in their political power. As they act they become more knowledgeable about what can be done. In addition, once they are involved, they come to depend less on actual results, but continue to act because they see action as necessary and right. With their actions congruent with their values, with their whole motivational system probably more integrated,[39] these activists acquire an increased sense of inner integrity.[40]

For effective action, it is important to approach and engage in dialogue with members of the media, writers, politicians, and others who can reach the public. But the potential influence of every person must be made clear: in speaking to others and influencing others' knowledge and ways of thinking; in initiating behavior that benefits others, changes the self, and brings about reciprocal actions that build connections; in initiating cross-cutting relations; and so on.

38. S. Moscovici, "Toward a Theory of Conversion Behavior," in *Current Issues in Social Psychology,* ed. L. Berkowitz (New York: Academic Press, 1980).

39. Staub, *The Roots of Evil.*

40. M. G. Locatelli and R. R. Holt, "Antinuclear Activism, Psychic Numbing, and Mental Health," *International Journal of Mental Health* (special issue, "Mental Health Implications of Life in the Nuclear Age," ed. M. Schwebel) 15 (1986): 143–162.

THE SELF AND ITS RELATIONSHIP TO OTHERS An individual's embeddedness in a group can reduce the person's likelihood of responding to the groups harming those in subgroups as well as to official policies that are potentially destructive. There has been recent recognition that the valuing of autonomous selves that characterizes Western thinking is not universal, but that various groups value and promote different forms of the development of identity and the self-concept. Some promote a self-definition that is more relational: other people are part of the self-concept, or connection to others is inherent in the self, or the boundaries of the self are fluid. Some authors in the past decade have suggested that women in our society have more relational selves.[41] Gilligan has also suggested that women's morality is based on care and responsibility, whereas males' is based on rules and logic.[42] Whether these differences are tied to gender or not, the possibility they suggest of different types of connections between self and others is important. In some Asian societies individual selves are less delineated, less autonomous, more inherently relational.[43]

Family and couples therapists stress that for people to function well in modern families good differentiation must exist between themselves and both people in their families of origin and their current mates. But those with autonomous, self-contained identities may have more difficulty in developing values that lead them to respond to the needs of other persons or to act to promote the social good.

On the other hand, people who have undifferentiated selves and are *embedded* in a group cannot arrive at an independent definition of reality or take action against a destructive course the group might be pursuing. The capacity to be separate is required for "group-

41. J. Surrey, *Self-in-Relation: A Theory of Women's Development* (Wellesley, Mass.: Stone Center, Wellesley College, 1985).

42. C. Gilligan, *In a Different Voice: Psychological Theory and Women's Development* (Cambridge: Harvard University Press, 1982).

43. J. R. Weiss, F. M. Rothbaum, and T. C. Blackburn, "Standing Out and Standing In: The Psychology of Control in America and Japan," *American Psychologist* 39 (1984): 955–969.

awareness"—self-awareness extended to one's group—and for critical consciousness, the capacity to hold views different from those
dominant in the group. It is also required for "critical loyalty," the
ability to oppose group policies and practices that one sees as destructive or as carrying a destructive potential. Japanese culture has
traditionally promoted connection between the individual and the
group—and kamikaze pilots may have been one result.

We need to create a third category to make sense of the findings
and theoretical ideas, that of the *embedded self*. As I define it, the
relational or *connected* self is less self-contained and more connected
to others than an autonomous self, but the person is differentiated
and flexible and can separate the self from others and from the group.
An embedded self is less differentiated than a connected self and its
identity more defined by group membership, whether the group is
the family or a nation.[44] The authoritarian child rearing and schools
that characterized Germany before World War II made it difficult to
develop either autonomous or connected selves and tended to give
rise to embedded selves.[45] We must strive to create cultures and institutions that promote the evolution of connected selves.

To mobilize people it is necessary to show the relationship of
issues, causes, and events to their selves, desires, values, and ideals.
But when we appeal to ideals, we must keep in mind the destruction
that has been wrought in the name of higher ideals. The improvement of the world must not become an abstraction; it must be
grounded in the welfare of individual human beings. In that frame-
work the future of children, the shared humanity of all people, the
satisfactions of connection and of helping others in need, the ideals
of peace and justice, can appeal to many.

It has been claimed that opposing the policies of the government
and the attitude of the majority is unpatriotic. But the true benefits
of such opposition to the group, how opposition serves important

44. Ervin Staub, "Individual and Group Selves, Motivation and Morality," in
Morality and the Self, ed. W. Edelstein and T. Wren (Cambridge: MIT Press, in press).
45. A. Miller, *For Your Own Good: Hidden Cruelty in Child-Rearing and the Roots
of Violence* (New York: Farrar, Straus, and Giroux, 1983); Staub, *The Roots of Evil.*

values, should be recognized. The mistreatment of groups of people within one's society, the mistreatment of people in other countries, the destruction of the environment, and the nuclear arms race seem diverse issues. What connects them is the valuing of persons and groups, the valuing of human welfare, and the great potential of bystanders to make a difference.

David Matas   *Chapter 11*

REMEMBERING THE HOLOCAUST

AUTHOR'S NOTE: My interest in genocide has arisen from a general human rights concern. I am a lawyer in private practice in Winnipeg, Manitoba, Canada, specializing in refugee law. Many of my clients are people who have fled attempted genocide. At the Canadian Commission of Inquiry on War Criminals, held in 1986, I represented the League for Human Rights of B'nai B'rith Canada as senior counsel at all public hearings.

I have written, with Susan Charendoff, *Justice Delayed: Nazi War Criminals in Canada* (Toronto: Summerhill Press, 1987).

Why should the world remember the Holocaust, the Nazi-perpetrated genocide of the Jews? This is a question that seems almost ridiculous to pose. One would think that it goes without saying that the past—and genocide in particular—should be remembered. Nonetheless, what one person takes from granted, another does not. This chapter examines the reasons for remembering the Holocaust.

An imperative reason for remembering is the contemporary rise of neo-Nazism. Although it is not an especially popular phenomenon, it indicates that the anti-Semitism that prompted the mass murders still exists. Moreover, it now often takes the form of denying that the Holocaust ever happened. Our remembering the past—affirming that it did indeed happen—relieves the victims of the burden of establishing the historical record.

Hate propaganda is becoming bolder and more pervasive, and indifference to it and to its consequences in the past only sows the seeds of future hatred. The activities of groups in the United States like the Aryan Nations and the Liberty Lobby and of people in Canada like Jim Keegstra, Ernst Zundel, John Ross Taylor, Donald Clarke Andrews, Robert Wayne Smith, and Malcolm Ross are the harvest of past indifference. When governments ignore the Holocaust, it becomes that much easier for those who would deny that it happened and would perpetuate its evil.

Although the crimes themselves were the work of a relatively few individuals, they were made possible by the passivity of whole populations. One task we must assume is to ensure that never again will a society in general remain passive in the face of mass murders organized by a few. To do this will require widespread education and a determined effort to remember history.

Education about the Holocaust belongs in the schools and in the history textbooks. Although extensive materials have been developed, many have been reluctant to use them. One program designed to overcome that reluctance has been that of the League for Human Rights of B'nai B'rith Canada, which offers to Canadian educators tours of the death camps of Europe, followed by a visit to Israel. The program, called "Holocaust and Hope," serves both an educational and a motivational purpose. Teachers return to their classrooms impelled by their experiences to pass on what they have seen and learned to their students.

The prosecution of Nazi war criminals can also serve an educational purpose. When the public learns of a particular crime committed during the course of the Holocaust, it makes concrete its overwhelming devastation. A trial, with daily media reporting, provides fresh insights into the Holocaust—its premises and its techniques. Nazi war crimes trials, of course, should not be conducted merely for publicity, but, rather, to bring mass murderers to justice. Once a trial is taking place, however, its educational value should not be overlooked. For instance, in Canada, during some trials, schoolchildren have been brought in to watch part of the proceedings.

Yet another reason for remembering the Holocaust is that soon all the perpetrators, all the surviving victims, all the witnesses, will be dead. Their memories must be recorded before it is too late. It is now forty-six years since the end of World War II. Those who were young adults then are now in their late sixties. As many survivors as possible should be interviewed and encouraged to recall their experiences. That has been done in order to prosecute Nazi war criminals, but there is another reason.

The survivors of the Holocaust represent the collective memory of those who died. Only the survivors can tell us who lived, who died, who helped, who hindered. Each survivor is a fount of information to be tapped. There are, of course, many memoirs, films, interviews, and recordings of survivors, but there still remains a tremendous work of documentation to be done. Yad Vashem in Israel serves as a repository of memories of the Holocaust. But though one repository in Israel is useful, it is not sufficient. The Holocaust should be remembered everywhere, not just in Israel.

In Winnipeg, my own city, the government of the province of Manitoba has erected on the grounds of the legislature a monument in the form of a stone Star of David. The names of all those who died in the Holocaust and who have surviving relatives in Manitoba are carved in the stone. That is an example of how a community can participate in remembering the Holocaust.

For remembrance to be truly effective, however, it should not be isolated from the rest of human experience. The Holocaust was in some respects unique: in its scope, its aims, its techniques; but genocide, incitement to genocide, and attempts at genocide are regettably all too common. If we dwell on the unique components of the Holocaust, if we do not learn its lessons and apply them to contemporary events, we will be "forgetting" the Holocaust in another sense. We must remember not only what happened but why and how it happened—the prevalent anti-Semitism, the use of hate propaganda to spread and deepen that anti-Semitism, the refusal, in the name of realpolitik, of the world community to object to state-sponsored anti-Semitism in Germany in the thirties, the failure of the world's nations to admit refugees trying to flee the oncoming Holocaust and then the Holocaust itself.

The story of the postwar reluctance to bring to justice many of the Nazi war criminals cannot be divorced from the story of the refusal of governments to help the Jews during the war. They are not two stories; they are two chapters in a continuing story. The Allies refused to bomb the camps or the railroads leading to them; they failed to provide ships and havens for refugees from Nazi Europe, to declare free ports, and to censure the Vatican for its behavior in relation to the Holocaust. That dismal record means that the world must make atonement. It must acknowledge its guilt by omission, its failure to act, which made the Holocaust possible.

Guilt for the Holocaust is shared worldwide because of all the people the nations of the world could have saved and did not. Canada must share this guilt because of its restrictive anti-Semitic immigration policy in place at the time. Of all the countries in the Western world, Canada's record was the worst.[1] Indeed, it was easier for a Nazi to come to Canada after the war than for a Jew to come during the war.

There have been counterparts to the Nazi Holocaust, for all its horrors. It was preceded by the Armenian genocide perpetrated in Turkey. It has been succeeded by the killing fields of Kampuchea, the mass killings in Uganda under Idi Amin and Obote, and the wholesale disappearances in Argentina. Lessons learned from the Holocaust could have helped us deter these mass murders, which continue to plague the world.

1. Irving Abella and Harold Troper, *Canada and the Jews of Europe, 1933–1948* (Toronto: Lester and Orpen Dennys, 1982), x.

Recent events in Indochina illustrate what happens both when we remember the Holocaust and act accordingly and when we do not. Many, for example, recalled the Holocaust in the case of the Vietnamese boat people in 1979. But in contrast, the lessons of the Holocaust have been forgotten or ignored in dealing with the Khmer Rouge of Cambodia.

The forced expulsion of ethnic Chinese from Vietnam was compared by many to the Nazi genocide of the Jews. S. Rajaratnam commented that the Vietnamese being cast adrift on the open seas was "a poor man's alternative to the gas chambers."[2] And U.S. vice president Walter Mondale was reminded of the failure of world governments meeting in 1938 in Evian, France, to find protection for Jewish refugees. More important, however, were the concrete actions that followed. A U.N. conference in Geneva in December 1978 resulted in various countries pledging to admit 82,350 Indochinese refugees over one year. By June 1, 1979, these commitments had increased to 125,000, and by July, to 260,000. The United States had doubled the number it would admit, 14,000 a month, and Canada had tripled its commitment.[3]

The citizens of Canada were well ahead of their government, however. At the time the Canadian government announced its willingness to take in Vietnamese boat people, it also set up a system of private sponsorship, whereby any corporation or group of five individuals could sponsor a refugee. Officials said that Canada would match, with government sponsorship, every refugee privately sponsored; the number was limited only by the willingness and ability of private persons to undertake sponsorship. But the response was far greater than the government had anticipated, and eventually it reneged on its commitment, saying it would match only 25,000 privately sponsored refugees, even if individuals sponsored more. After the Conservative government reduced its commitment, it was de-

2. Quoted in Helen Fein, *Congregational Sponsors of Indochinese Refugees in the United States, 1979–1982: Helping beyond Borders* (Rutherford, N.J.: Fairleigh Dickinson University Press, 1987), 45.

3. Ibid., 47.

feated in Parliament in December 1979. Its backtracking on matching became an election issue, with the opposition Liberals campaigning on a platform of full matching. When the Liberals won the subsequent election in early 1980, full matching was restored.

If the Vietnam story is heartening, the Cambodia story is not. There has been total inactivity in the face of the Khmer Rouge genocide. The West recognizes as the legal government of Cambodia a coalition that includes the Khmer Rouge. Cambodia and Western governments have signed and ratified the U.N. Genocide Convention, which obligates signatory states to prosecute and punish perpetrators of the crime of genocide. The Convention also allows any signatory state to bring before the World Court in The Hague any other signatory state that fails in this obligation. The Cambodian government has prosecuted no one for the Khmer Rouge genocide, yet no Western government has invoked the U.N. Convention to bring Cambodia before the World Court.

Zbigniew Brzezinski, national security adviser under U.S. president Jimmy Carter, described American policy in Cambodia by saying, "I encouraged the Chinese to encourage Pol Pot." Richard Cohen, a *Washington Post* columnist, wrote, "In effect U.S. policy remained ever thus," and he likened the situation to the Allies' supporting Hitler after World War II if he had survived and continued to fight the Russians.[4] Hurst Hannum made a similar comment. He wrote that the reasoning that has led to other Asian states supporting the Khmer Rouge would have permitted Hitler to remain in power after the war, had Nazi Germany not been so thoroughly defeated.[5]

The United States has been slow to bring Nazi criminals in America to justice, one reason being the extensive recruitment and use of Nazis in the cold war. The U.S. Office of Special Investigation, devoted to identifying and tracking down Nazi war criminals, was not established until 1978. Canada has been even slower. Its war crimes

4. "U.S. on the Side of Genocide," *Institute for the Study of Genocide Newsletter,* no. 4 (Fall 1989): 3, from Richard Cohen, "On the Side of Genocide," *Washington Post,* September 24, 1989.

5. "Cambodian Genocide," *Human Rights Quarterly* 2 (1989): 137.

legislation was not passed until 1987. Britain has yet to begin pros-
ecutions.

If we ignore the Holocaust now, we compound the ignominy of
the past, the failure of the world's nations to help the Jews. We make
a black record even blacker. But we cannot hermetically seal off Nazi
war crimes in the past. What we remember of them determines our
future. Remembering the Holocaust and changing our behavior in
light of its lessons deals with the past—and also makes a statement
of what we are, what we want to become.

Remembering the Holocaust is a measure of atonement. But
atonement requires more than simply remembering; it requires action. We must prosecute those Nazi murderers who remain free to
this day. We must bring to justice the Khmer Rouge responsible for
the killing fields of Kampuchea. Remembering and acting are inex-
tricably linked.

When we remember the Holocaust, the effort is, above all, for
humanity. What we remember says something about ourselves, about
our willingness to accept responsibility. The message we give by forgetting is that mass murder is acceptable. Is that the message we
want to leave with history?

Katharine R. Bigelow　　　　　　　　　　　　　　　*Chapter 12*

A CAMPAIGN TO
DETER GENOCIDE:
THE BAHÁ'Í EXPERIENCE

AUTHOR'S NOTE: Since 1985 I have been a representative of the National Spiritual Assembly of the Bahá'ís of the United States in the U.S. Congress, at the White House, in the State Department, and in the Immigration and Naturalization Service. The Bahá'ís keep government agencies informed about the status of the Bahá'ís in Iran and other countries and about Iranian Bahá'í refugees who have fled persecution by the Islamic regime. The Bahá'ís testified at hearings on the persecution of the Iranian Bahá'ís before the House of Representatives subcommittees on Human Rights and on Immigration, Refugees, and International Law. In 1989 we worked with the American Bar Association on a report and a resolution condemning human rights violations in Iran. During the last few years, I have given numerous newspaper and radio interviews, spoken publicly on the Iranian Bahá'í situation, and taken part in the Harvard Law School Human Rights series.

I believe the case of the Iranian Bahá'ís is both a model and a source of hope to the many oppressed and persecuted peoples of the world. That the

Islamic Republic of Iran, which has vociferously claimed its immunity from the impact of public opinion, should react to the repeated appeals of governments, of the United Nations, and of the media by mitigating the egregious treatment of its largest religious minority gives us renewed optimism that the light of publicity can be a beacon exposing the atrocities of other governments and shaming them into behaving according to universally accepted human rights standards.

Since 1979 the Islamic Republic of Iran has conducted a systematic campaign of persecution against the Bahá'í community, designed to eliminate the Bahá'ís as a religious minority in Iran. The persecution has encompassed physical, economic, and social intimidation and has taken many forms, including summary executions, torture, arbitrary imprisonment, denial of education and employment, and arbitrary seizure of homes and possessions. All Bahá'í community assets have been confiscated. All Bahá'í holy places have been seized and desecrated, the most important of them being demolished. In almost every case the authorities told the Bahá'ís that the campaign against them would cease if only they would abandon their religion—an offer that demonstrated conclusively that religion is the basis for their persecution.[1]

The current wave of persecutions against the Iranian Bahá'í community should not be viewed as an isolated phenomenon—a recent development created by the Islamic Revolution. Since the inception of their religion in the middle of the last century, the Bahá'ís of Iran have lived in a climate of constant repression characterized by frequent outbreaks of violence and bloodshed. In the 1840s and 1850s, over 20,000 Bahá'ís were branded as heretics of the Muslim religion and were put to death in circumstances of appalling cruelty. Under subsequent regimes, including those of the Pahlavis, the persecution continued, often accompanied by bloodshed.[2]

    1. Bahá'í International Community, *Persecution of the Bahá'ís of Iran, 1979–1986: A 7-Year Campaign to Eliminate a Religious Minority* (New York: Bahá'í International Community, December 1986), 5.
    2. Bahá'í International Community, *The Bahá'ís of Iran: A Report on the Perse-*

The majority of modern-day executions, over 190, took place between 1979 and 1984. As of December 1988, 210 Bahá'ís had been killed by the Iranian authorities, but with no more recorded between then and March 1991. Thousands were imprisoned in the early 1980s, with an average of 750 per year being imprisoned between 1983 and 1985. Fewer than 10 remained in prisons in March 1991, however.

The Constitution of the Islamic Republic of Iran, which recognizes and protects the Jewish, Christian, and Zoroastrian minorities in that country, denies recognition to Iran's largest religious minority, the followers of the Bahá'í Faith. As a result, Iran's 300,000 Bahá'ís are deprived of any form of protection under law and suffer continuous infringements of their fundamental human rights.[3] They are not permitted to organize, to practice their religion, to hold property, to operate religious schools, to send their children to universities, or to emigrate legally. Thousands have been dismissed from their jobs, and many have been denied pensions, insurance, and other earned benefits.

THE INITIAL RESPONSE

In 1990, there were approximately 5 million Bahá'ís worldwide, with about 70,000 in Europe, 110,000 in the United States, 2.3 million in South Asia, and 1.3 million in Africa. Over the past decade between 20,000 and 30,000 Bahá'ís have escaped from Iran. These refugees have resettled worldwide from Brazil to Australia. About 10,000 have resettled in the United States.

When the Islamic Revolution began in Iran in the fall of 1978, the Bahá'ís throughout the rest of the world were deeply concerned that government-sponsored persecution would lead to the deaths of as many as 20,000 of the 350,000 Iranian Bahá'ís. But the Iranian

---

cution of a Religious Minority (New York: Bahá'í International Community, June 1981), 1.

   3. Ibid.

government eventually realized that its initial campaign to eliminate the elected leadership of the Bahá'í community, hoping thereby to precipitate mass recantation, had failed and that it would have to kill hundreds of thousands to eradicate the community. Twelve years later, it is clear that the decision to publicize the regime's campaign to eliminate the Bahá'ís helped save thousands of lives and limit the number of executions to 210.

At first Bahá'í leaders were unsure whether to use a quiet, behind-the-scenes approach or to publicize the persecutions. At the outset of the revolution they decided not to seek publicity because they feared that publicity would do them greater harm. But the Bahá'í international community, representing over 140 national communities, eventually used several means to inform and educate governments, international organizations, the press, the academic world, and ordinary citizens. The effort helped prevent a massacre of the Iranian Bahá'í community. The Bahá'í Faith, which has no clergy, administers its affairs through an elected structure that includes an international governing body and 150 national and 20,000 local governing bodies called assemblies. These were the institutions that coordinated activities and contacts with the press and their respective governments.

Credit for the prevention of further genocide should be given primarily to the Iranian Bahá'ís themselves. Despite the extent of the persecution and the Islamic regime's repeated offers to cease persecuting those who recanted and returned to the Muslim faith, fewer than a hundred Bahá'ís did so during the decade. By tenet of faith, Bahá'ís may not deny or recant their faith, even under the threat of death.

Recognition must be given also to the Iranism Muslim citizens who provided protection and assistance to Bahá'ís. Without the help of these Iranians, many Bahá'ís would have suffered more deeply from the persecution by the Islamic regime.

INTERNATIONAL RESPONSE

On September 10, 1980, the U.N. Sub-Commission on Prevention of Discrimination and Protection of Minorities expressed in a resolution "its profound concern for the safety of the recently arrested members of the National Administrative Council of the Bahá'ís of Iran, and that of all members of this community, both as individuals and collectively."[4] Since 1982 the U.N. Human Rights Commission has passed resolutions condemning human rights violations in Iran and mentioning the Bahá'ís as a specific victimized group. Resolutions on Iran have been passed by the U.N. General Assembly each year since 1985. In January 1990, the U.N. special representative on Iran, Reynaldo Galindo Pohl, issued a report on his findings of human rights violations in Iran after he heard testimony and visited Teheran. In it, he bore out each of the claims the Bahá'ís had made for the past decade.

Bahá'ís in various countries have kept their foreign ministeries informed of events in Iran by providing timely and accurate information about the persecutions. Several national parliaments, including those of Germany, Australia, Canada, and Fiji, have issued resolutions condemning the treatment of the Bahá'í religious minority.

When the Bahá'ís decided to publicize the persecutions and to seek the assistance of government leaders, those in the United States realized they needed professional advice on how to reach policy and decision makers. How could an organization that could not afford an expensive media campaign of television and newspaper advertisements make its voice heard? Initially, the American Bahá'ís enlisted the help of the public relations firm Hill and Knowlton. The agency arranged for the Bahá'ís to meet with the Human Rights and Refugee bureaus at the State Department and to contact congressional offices that have participated in human rights activities in the past.

4. United Nations, Economic and Social Council, Commission on Human Rights, Sub-Commission on Prevention of Discrimination and Protection of Minorities, *Report of the Sub-Commission on the Prevention of Discrimination and Protection of Minorities on Its Thirty-third Session*, E/CN.4/1413 E/CN.4/Sub.2/459, October 13, 1980.

In 1982 when Representative Don Bonker, then chairman of the Subcommittee on Human Rights of the Foreign Affairs Committee in the House of Representatives, decided to invite the Bahá'ís to testify at a hearing on religious persecution, Hill and Knowlton helped stage the event by creating displays of graphic materials and contacting the press. The American Bahá'ís also drew on the professional skills of public relations firms at hearings in 1984 and 1988 before the same subcommittee. The firms also helped the Bahá'ís compare Senate and House concurrent resolutions condemning the Iranian government's treatment of the Bahá'ís, and these were passed by Congress in 1982, 1984, 1988, and 1990. The American Bahá'ís now employ the public relations firm Fleishman Hillard to provide technical advice and expertise.

Some seventeen hundred local Bahá'í assemblies in the United States have contacted their local newspapers. Thus, in addition to coverage in the national press such as the *New York Times* and the *Washington Post,* the story of the Iranian Bahá'ís has been repeated in thousands of news articles, personal accounts by refugees, and letters to the editor. Local Bahá'ís visited the papers and wrote to their representatives in Congress urging their support for the congressional resolutions. Others drew on friendships with members of Congress or other government figures. They thereby formed a grass-roots constituency for the Iranian Bahá'ís.

Congress's response to the pleas for help has been impressive. Because the Bahá'í community is so small, those in Congress who have supported the Bahá'ís have done so without thought of political benefit. Rather, theirs has been a human response to suffering that has brought out the best in everyone. The fundamental American value of religious liberty has been reaffirmed.

RECENT EVENTS

In an article in May 1990 responding to the passage by the U.S. Senate of its fourth resolution condemning Iran's continued persecution and denial of rights to the Bahá'ís, the government-sponsored newspaper, the *Jumhuri Islami,* stated, "Although the existence of the misguided Bahá'í sect in Iran is going toward extinction, the Americans, particularly the Zionist wing of the government, do not let go of the remnants of this group of spies or deceived individuals and continue to shed crocodile tears for them."[5] Thus, although the manifest threat of imprisonment and death is less, the Islamic Republic of Iran continues to reiterate its goal of the annihilation of the Bahá'í community.

Nevertheless, there has been improvement in the treatment of individual Bahá'ís in recent years. Children may now attend primary and secondary school, although no students may attend the universities. Businessmen have been allowed to open their shops. Some Bahá'ís have obtained visas to travel outside the country.

Perhaps another indication of a different direction by a government institution was a ruling by a court in Qazvin. The court upheld the right of a Bahá'í plaintiff against a Muslim business associate who had refused to honor a contractual agreement on the grounds that he was dealing with a Bahá'í. The court stated that noncriminal Bahá'ís could engage in business and that no one could oppose them. This decision by a lower court may be indicative of a gradual lessening of the harsher aspects of the persecution.

The Bahá'í community as a whole, however, is without legal protection and is denied civil and political rights. The process of improvement for individuals could be reversed at any time. The Bahá'í international community remains vigilant and continues to use the United Nations, the U.S. Congress, and the communications media to keep the public informed about the persecution and to let the Iranian government know that the world has not forgotten the Bahá'ís.

That the Bahá'í case is so straightforward has been an important component of the overall success of the publicity campaign. Over the years it has been established unequivocally that the Bahá'ís have committed no acts of sedition against the state. The Iranian govern-

5. "Bahá'ísm in Iran 'Is Going Towards Complete Extinction,'" *International Iran Times* (Washington, D.C.), May 11, 1990, 6.

ment has produced no evidence against the Bahá'ís, and their trials
have clearly been shams. The Bahá'ís have easily persuaded the world
of the veracity of their claim that the Iranian Bahá'ís are being persecuted for religious reasons alone.

The combination of professional advice by public relations firms,
contacts with government figures, press, and human rights organizations, and the integrity of the cause itself has led to the remarkable
results of the decade-long campaign to protect the Bahá'ís in Iran.

Vratislav Pechota   *Chapter 13*

ESTABLISHING CRIMINAL
RESPONSIBILITY AND
JURISDICTION FOR GENOCIDE

AUTHOR'S NOTE: My interest in human rights grows out of my own experience and deep personal beliefs. During World War II, our family lived in
Nazi-occupied Bohemia, and my father spent the war years in a German
prison. Our Jewish friends and neighbors were all sent to Theresienstadt to
be later transported to places like Auschwitz, from which there was no return. Many non-Jewish fellow citizens shared their fate.

As an international lawyer, who participated in the work of legal bodies
of the United Nations from 1953 to 1968, I was involved in the preparation
of the Covenants on Human Rights and other international instruments. I
have written on international law and human rights and am preparing a
book on "The Genocide Convention and Beyond." I am currently associated
with Columbia University where I teach courses on Soviet legal institutions
and approaches to international law, and serve as assistant director of the
Parker School of Foreign and Comparative Law.

This chapter discusses the extent of individual responsibility for genocide and the jurisdiction of national courts according to the 1948 Genocide Convention. It also addresses the issue of international jurisdiction, including the feasibility of creating an international tribunal for genocide.

THE GENOCIDE CONVENTION

On November 25, 1988, the United States became the ninety-ninth nation expressing its consent to be bound by the Convention on the Prevention and Punishment of the Crime of Genocide.

The U.S. ratification was a logical consequence of an integral design to make the prohibition of the crime of genocide truly universal. That prohibition was conceived and formulated under the impact of the enormity of the wrong wrought by the Nazis in the Holocaust; its only purpose is to prevent or punish any future occurrences.

The Convention embodies international consensus regarding the ways to achieve its purpose. It defines the proscribed conduct and places duty on the contracting states to prevent genocide and if the crime is committed, to punish its perpetrators. Guilty persons are to be prosecuted, whether they are constitutionally responsible rulers, public officials, or private individuals. The Convention requires states to enact legislation to make genocide a crime under their laws. The parties to the Convention pledge themselves to grant extradition in accordance with their laws and treaties in force. Persons charged with genocide are to be brought for trial before a court of the country in which they committed the crime or before a competent international tribunal. Disputes relating to the interpretation, application, and fulfillment of the Convention, including those concerning the responsibility of a state for genocide, are to be submitted to the International Court of Justice. The Convention expressly states that the United Nations is competent to take appropriate action to deter and suppress acts of genocide.

ASSESSING RESPONSIBILITY

International law places emphasis on criminal responsibility of individual perpetrators of the crime of genocide. Charges against states can be adjudicated only by the International Court of Justice as noncriminal contentious matters. The well-established doctrine of sovereign immunity effectively bars the jurisdiction of domestic courts over acts of genocide committed by foreign states.

The Nuremberg Trial provides the most significant legal precedent for individual criminal responsibility for genocide. Its judgment clearly established the supremacy of international law in terms of individual responsibility for the proscribed offenses by stating that individuals have international duties that transcend the national obligations of obedience imposed by the individual state.

The Genocide Convention (Art. 4) introduces the concept of strict criminal responsibility of officials by providing that "persons committing genocide . . . shall be punished, whether they are constitutionally responsible rulers, public officials or private individuals." The concept apparently eliminates the defenses of sovereign immunity and official position. It is not clear, however, whether and to what extent it makes inadmissible such affirmative defenses as command of law or superior orders. It certainly does not prevent the court from considering defenses such as coercion or the impossibility of refusing to act, which could play an important part in determining the responsibility of the accused.

The defense of superior order poses an especially difficult question. It rests on the demands of discipline in the bureaucratic and military hierarchies of the state. A soldier's dilemma in the question of obedience (on the one hand, he may be liable to be shot by a court-martial if he disobeys an order and, on the other, to be hanged by a judge and jury if he obeys it) has not been satisfactorily resolved in the Genocide Convention. Until the principle that superior orders do not free an accused of responsibility for an international crime is transformed into national law and spelled out in terms that leave no doubt of the duty to refuse to obey an order to perform a criminal act, it may be impossible to enforce in practice the principle of strict criminal liability embraced by the Convention.

In the absence of internationally agreed rules concerning defenses, it will be up to the tribunal to determine whether the justifying and excusing grounds are valid and to give them meaning and scope.

THE ISSUE OF JURISDICTION

The central issue to be resolved in each case is that of the competent court. According to the Genocide Convention, the court of the country where an act of genocide has been committed has the power to hear and decide on charges against individual perpetrators.

Domestic courts exercise jurisdiction over genocide in accordance with national law and enjoy discretion in respect of the procedure to be followed. No effort has been made to harmonize rules concerning details of proscribed conduct, admissible defenses, and sentencing policy.

The Genocide Convention does not provide for a case in which a state fails to bring those accused of an act of genocide to trial. Does such a state forfeit its jurisdiction? Can the perpetrators be tried before the courts of another country?

The territorial principle embodied in the Genocide Convention is useful to governments that are prepared to institute proceedings against responsible individuals in order to distance themselves from the policies of an overthrown regime under whose authority the crime was perpetrated. This took place in 1979 in Equatorial Guinea, where the new government created a special military tribunal and tried deposed president Francisco Macias Nguema and ten of his associates on charges of genocide and mass murder involving violations of both domestic and international law. Also Bangladesh claimed territorial jurisdiction to adjudicate the charges of genocide committed in East Pakistan.

On the other hand, the same principle proved unsatisfactory in the Eichmann case, in which the Israeli court was unable to invoke the territorial basis for its jurisdiction because the offense was committed outside of Israel. For this reason, the trial court relied not on the territorial principle but on the jurisdictional principles of passive personality and protection of vital state interests. According to this doctrine, it was irrelevant that the state of Israel did not exist at the date of the commission of the crime: the right of the injured group to punish offenders derived directly from the crime committed against it, and only its want of sovereignty denied it the power to punish; if the injured group of people achieved political sovereignty in any territory, it might exercise such sovereignty to enforce its natural right to punish the offender who injured it. In addition, according to the Israeli Law for the Prevention and Punishment of Genocide, 5710/1950, any person who has committed outside Israel an act that is an offense under the law may be prosecuted and punished in Israel as if he had committed the act in Israel. At the appellate stage, the Supreme Court of Israel upheld these bases of Israeli jurisdiction and, in addition, invoked the principle of universal jurisdiction that afforded the state of Israel the right to try the appellant.

Universal jurisdiction implies the authority of any state to punish certain crimes regardless of where and by whom they have been committed. No links of territory or nationality are required for prosecuting these cases. The Genocide Convention does not expressly forbid application of this jurisdictional principle.

A trend can be observed in recent years to replace the territorial principle by the principle of limited universal jurisdiction. Several conventions dealing with the suppression and punishment of international crimes have adopted the rule that any state in whose territory an individual alleged to have committed an international crime is present is bound either to try or to extradite him.

If universal jurisdiction is indeed the wave of the future, it may be expedient to adopt it as common denominator and make it applicable to the crime of genocide. This may be achieved without changing the Genocide Convention. The principle of universal jurisdiction can be applied exceptionally as a matter of customary law, which provides an alternative to the Genocide Convention. This approach, however, should not be allowed to displace territorial jurisdiction; it can merely create an option. It may be exercised in cases in which the territorial state knowingly forfeits its jurisdiction by failing to bring those accused of an act of genocide to trial. Perhaps a rule should be established that the crime to be punished must have some link to the state claiming jurisdiction. In order to diminish the potential for abuse and provide a screen against propagandist resort to court, additional guarantees should be created. For example, it could be agreed that if the accused is brought to trial before a tribunal of a third country, the trial court should include a judge from the jurisdiction of the accused.

No international tribunal having criminal jurisdiction over genocide has been created, and it is unlikely that agreement can be secured soon on the establishment of a permanent international criminal court. All past efforts foundered mainly on the opposition of the Soviet Union, which held that the proposal was contrary to the principles of sovereignty and independence of states and would open the door to intervention in the internal affairs of states. The Soviet Union is now reassessing its policies with regard to international mechanisms enforcing human rights, including the prohibition of genocide. This makes the general acceptance of international jurisdiction a practical possibility.

A new effort, if made, should be undertaken on a limited scale and restricted to genocide only, and it should not aim at the overthrow of the existing system of enforcement through national courts. It should create a stand-by mechanism to be put to work only when there is sufficient support for an international judicial action. The mechanism should be independent, effective, and universal, and it should be used sparingly. It could consist of procedures enabling the creation of ad hoc bodies rather than of permanent institutions.

One possibility is to create, within the United Nations, a standby complement comprising a commission of inquiry (indicting authority), a prosecuting attorney, and a tribunal.

The commission of inquiry appointed on a case-by-case basis by the Security Council or the General Assembly would gather and examine evidence of the alleged offense and determine if there were adequate and plausible grounds to bring the charge and proceed to trial. The indicting authority would submit its conclusion to the Security Council. The case would proceed to trial if the Council consented. The Council resolution conferring jurisdiction would also contain the terms of reference of the tribunal.

The prosecuting attorney or attorneys, appointed by the president of the Security Council after consultations with the Council's members, would present evidence at the trial and conduct the prosecution in court. The ad hoc tribunal would be set up by the Security Council or the General Assembly, or both, and its activities would be governed by a Model Statute and Rules of an International Tribunal for the Trial of Persons Accused of the Crime of Genocide, to be worked out by the International Law Commission and approved by the General Assembly. The members of the tribunal would be appointed by the Security Council. In turn, the tribunal would appoint the clerk of the court and any other necessary officers. A joint registrar arrangement could be made with the International Court of Justice at The Hague.

The accused should be entitled to counsel of his own choosing at all stages of the trial proceedings, as well as to other rights guaranteed by Article 14 of the International Covenant on Civil and Political Rights.

The system should protect against the possibility of a group of states organizing to confer jurisdiction for purposes of propaganda or political embarrassment of other states.

ENFORCING THE PROHIBITION OF GENOCIDE

Questions of substantive rules merge with questions of the machinery by which the prohibition of genocide is to be enforced. Although it must be assumed that the commitment to comply with the Convention's provisions has been undertaken in good faith, the international community must know whether these provisions are consistently and fairly applied.

It may be difficult to obtain agreement to the establishment of a new standing mechanism, similar to the Human Rights Committee set up under the International Covenant on Civil and Political Rights, for monitoring compliance with the Genocide Convention. An additional protocol to the Genocide Convention would be required to put such a proposal into effect. Therefore, the task should be entrusted to the existing U.N. bodies having general authority to deal with matters of serious political and humanitarian concern.

It may be desirable, however, to develop certain ancillary procedures outside the U.N. structure—for instance, for the exchange of views on ways of implementing the Convention and for recommending appropriate measures if the need arises. These procedures need not be laborious in order to be efficacious. Consultation, held at regular intervals, of permanent representatives of the states accredited to the European Office of the United Nations in Geneva could be an appropriate setup.

The international effort to prevent and punish genocide can be effectively assisted by countries situated in the vicinity of a scene of genocide. Neighboring countries are in a unique position to warn of impending genocide and to help its victims. They are almost inevitably involved by reason of their having to share the burden of the refugee problem and other consequences. The U.N. General Assembly should adopt a resolution defining the role of neighboring countries in situations involving genocide and calling upon them to signal acts of genocide and secure evidence. Perhaps the U.N. secretary-general should be designated as the recipient of any such information. Unless the neighboring country requested that the communication be kept confidential, the secretary-general could decide to pass on the information to the competent U.N. organ with or without his own observations.

In order to mitigate the consequences of the crime, there should be set up, preferably within the United Nations, an international mechanism for the compensation, restitution, and resettlement of groups victimized by acts of genocide. The functions of the mechanism could include providing legal assistance and financial and material help to the victims.

DATE

NOV − 3 1993

FEB 2 8 1995

MAR 1 4 1995

MAR 2 8 1995   MAR 2

APR 1 7 1995

MAY 5/95

16 1997

DEC APR 0 1999

Brodart Co.   Cat. # 55 137 001